This book is about m
oneself, for all with whom ...., and for the
wonderful world in which we and so many other creatures find
ourselves. It is original, interdisciplinary and a great read – not
least because the author cites his own experiences as examples
of living and learning, warmly commends 'best practice', and
knows how, when and where we can make a contribution to
creating the best world imaginable.

- ANN LOADES, CBE

Samie's ability to both intellectually and intuitively pinpoint the
core details of what is important about humanity on this planet
while making connections between business and life makes his
book an exceptional read.

- CÉLINE COUSTEAU

This book is for conscious leaders who are here to change the
world. It is the blueprint for greater consciousness as we know
it, and what that means for individuals and society.

- HELEN PARKER FRSA

Insightful and inspirational, this epic book explores values
and culture from both a business and individual perspective.
On offer is wisdom and encouragement to step up and face
humanity's complex modern challenges and collectively choose
a better way of working and living in a post-COVID world.

- VICTORIA BRESSAN

Samie, thank you for being the voice for humanity.

- SANDY MAY

#Time4Humanity

Samie Al-Achrafi

Contents

About Samie

S amie is recognised as one of the world's leading voices on values and culture change. He has won a host of accolades including Most Visionary Business Transformation CEO, Game Changer of the Year and Most Influential CEO of the Year.

His career spans six continents, working with governments and organisations around the world to create high-performance cultures underpinned by values. In 2019, he presented a TED talk on *Why Business Needs Our Humanity* and created the hashtag #time4humanity, which brought the subject to the forefront of leaders' hearts and minds.

As the founder and CEO of Marmalade Fish, Samie leads a team of world-class facilitators and coaches to bring humanity to business, with a reach of over one million people in 2020. Marmalade Fish was the first certified B Corporation in the GCC, and has been named Best Organisational Change Consultancy and Change Management Company of the Year.

Samie gained a double first-class honours degree in philosophy and theology with a specialisation in ethics from the University of

Durham, and a master's degree in management (with distinction) from the University of London. His passion is aviation and he hopes one day to own a retired 747! Samie loves exploring nature trails while listening to podcasts. He is a reiki master and regularly participates in neurofeedback training to access the full range of brainwaves and states of consciousness, delta being his favourite.

Samie is a Fellow of the RSA, and a Chartered Fellow of the CIPD and CMI. He is also an NLP practitioner, executive and systemic coach, and assessor with the British Psychological Society.

@samiealachrafi
www.samiealachrafi.com

humanity

noun

1. human beings collectively;
2. compassionate, sympathetic or generous behaviour or disposition: the quality or state of being humane.

Humanity is defined by our essentially human qualities of feeling love, compassion and empathy, seeking connection and community, being creative, exercising free will and **not** functioning like a robot or machine.

The word comes from the Latin *humanitas* for 'human nature, kindness'.

Being human is a given. Keeping our humanity is a choice.

Dedicated to humanity, with reverence to wise elders past, present and emerging.

Where Are We Now?

Disasters seem to be winning right now.

The common thread running through learning methodologies that exist today is the focus on learning by reflecting on the experiences of the past. Yet when working with leadership teams in business, government and civil society, we see leaders facing new challenges that require them not only to reflect on the past, but to sense and actualise emerging future opportunities.

The question then becomes, how to create a new methodology that enables humanity to scry the future, as it lies embedded within the present, and use the resulting insights to guide our decisions.

The ability to see the implications of the emerging future has long been an important skill, but given the urgency of today's challenges, it is now more crucial than ever. There are plenty of historical examples that demonstrate what happens when we respond to a crisis using an old-world template, and fail to pay attention to all the hidden aspects of a current situation that do not conform and will thus negatively affect the outcome. Not only does such an approach not solve the problem, but it also keeps society stuck in a loop in which the same old patterns are continually recreated. We have reached crisis point, where addressing new-world problems with old-world thinking is no longer tenable.

Many things in our shared reality indicate that we are going through a transitional period, where it seems that something is on the way out and something else, still indistinct, is being born. The unconscious ways we have been living have become unsustainable and are breaking down. In this century, sleepwalking has been happening on a global scale.

The heavy-handed, top-down way that governments worldwide addressed the coronavirus crisis – effectively crashing the old system – may in the end have made them the unwitting agency of a necessary transformation in the evolution of our species. They may have been attempting to subvert and counteract the deeper changes that are already awakening part of the consciousness of humanity with their efforts to impose an even more unconscious, unnatural system on us. Yet let us hope their actions cannot ultimately succeed, and have instead pushed us all to the point where we are challenged to change ourselves. If there is one thing that history has taught us, it is that humanity has persevered through hardship by remembering and appealing to our finer nature, and by coming together collectively to rebuild the world anew on that basis.

Today, we find ourselves at a moment of choice. A choice of whether to accept unquestioningly the solutions that the system big players are proposing, or to awaken to the humane alternative and retain the natural human love for our own personal freedoms.

This book is about enlightened leadership. It is offered as a mosaic of ideas for leaders – that is, anyone, anywhere who is willing to step up and lead us into a fulfilling and meaningful future. Through an examination of past, present and emerging constructs, it invites us to consider our humanity, and what will be required of ourselves and our relations with others if we are to build that shining future.

In Part One, we begin with the human experience of work. We remind ourselves of the important roles played by embedded values and an intentional culture, and we start to examine the traditional notion of success in business and society. As the layers of our working life are peeled away, we spend time in Part Two exploring conscious leadership and gaining a deeper understanding of our collective citizenship on earth. We discover alternative worldviews and ways of being, addressing some of the most pressing issues of our time. In Part Three, we turn from the outer to the inner world, asking how our own state of mind and being can help to make a difference when it comes to contributing to the creation of the best world we can imagine.

COVID-19 has been described as a once-in-a-century event. The meaning of the word 'catastrophe' in ancient Greek is 'turning point'. It is time for this world ship, which has been steaming along in a certain direction, to stop and alter its course. It will take a while to turn her around – probably several generations – but this is the moment when humanity must come together and start to make that shift. If we can do this, I believe that within a decade or two we can usher in an enduring golden age for our world.

Part One – The Unconscious Past

The Value of Values

Open your arms to change but
don't let go of your values.
– Dalai Lama

Economist Milton Friedman once advised that the only duty of a corporation is to maximise return on its investment. It turns out this was poor advice.

Now, more than ever, employees are searching for meaning and purpose in their work. That does not mean everyone wants to work for a company whose sole mission is to 'do good', but most people want to work for a company that knows what it stands for, and what it values – a company that can be trusted not to behave in corrupt or shady ways.

What is a 'value'?
Values
n: principles that help one decide what is right and wrong, what is important in life, and thus how to act in various situations.

The values held by a person or social group reflect or constitute an emotional investment in a set of beliefs (either for or against something).

Ethics

n: a set of articulated moral principles governing a person's or group's behaviour, or the conduct of an activity.

Ethics tend to be codified into a formal system, set of rules or standards that govern the conduct of members of a profession.

These principles, and the practices in which they are embedded, may require careful scrutiny and evaluation from time to time.

How good people let bad things happen

Countless organisations have espoused values of 'integrity' and 'transparency'. In fact, Booz Allen Hamilton and the Aspen Institute found that of the 89% of companies with a written corporate values statement, 90% specified ethical conduct as a principle.

Yet trust in business is at an all-time low. Consider financial institutions – over the years, we have witnessed insider trading, the subprime mortgage crisis, sanctions breaches, the LIBOR scandal, money laundering, and the illegal funding of drug cartels, human traffickers and terrorist organisations. It seemed as though banks would do anything to drive shareholder value upwards. Capital owners benefitted from the short-term gains, while senior executives were largely not held accountable, with the exception of an occasional knighthood being removed. The fallout, however, resulted in nationalised debt, with years of collapsed and stagnated share prices. To take just one example, the UK government ploughed £20.3 billion into Lloyds during the global financial crisis, and the company then went on to pay out an eye-watering £21.8 billion in claims for mis-selling PPI.

Society is profoundly unimpressed by endless corporate claims to uphold certain values in mission statements that are blatantly hypocritical. As if values are mere words without any actual connotations, when in fact such implications are always systemic; they run through every single aspect of the company ethos.

If business is all about people, how is it that good people let such things happen? In a report commissioned by the Chartered Management Institute (CMI) entitled *The Moral DNA of Performance*, the authors showed that there are differences between individuals' sense of ethics at home and at work. It is as though we temporarily check out our humanity when we swipe our access cards to enter work, and regain human agency when we leave the building.

Joe Garner, former head of HSBC UK, did some research into the ethics of banking, and those of HSBC in particular, with the intention of understanding how to do the right thing in business. He concluded that, 'The blindingly simple insight is that in our personal lives we make decisions guided by principles, as well as the consideration of rules. But when we come to work, we create an environment where we can disable the human part.' Several investment bankers reported the ability to turn off emotions to achieve goals in the years leading up to the global financial crisis. It was not fearlessness they experienced – it was 'non-caringness'. In other words, the absence of humanity.

Wells Fargo proclaimed that, 'Our ethics are the sum of all the decisions each of us makes every day. If you want to find out how strong a company's ethics are, don't listen to what its people say. Watch what they do.' And yet US federal regulators found that Wells Fargo employees secretly created over two million unauthorised bank and credit-card accounts. Employees were encouraged to order credit cards for pre-approved customers without their consent, and to use their own contact information when filling out requests to prevent customers from discovering the fraud.

Employees also created fraudulent checking and savings accounts, a process that sometimes involved the movement of money out of legitimate accounts. The creation of these additional products was made possible in part through a process known as 'pinning'. By setting the client's pin to '0000', bankers were able to control client accounts, and to enrol them in programmes such as online banking.

John Stumpf, the then CEO of Wells Fargo, claimed that the problem was not due to the bank's culture – it was the work of a few unethical employees. 'The one percent who did it wrong, whom we fired – terminated – in no way reflect our culture,' he said.

If you enter 'recent corporate scandals' into a search engine, you will get more than eight million hits. Volkswagen's 'Dieselgate' is one of the most systemic and damaging examples of a business focusing on efficiency and financial return while deceiving its stakeholders. Michael Horn, the then CEO of Volkswagen US, offered an apology for Volkswagen's use of a software program that served to defeat the regular emissions-testing regime. Asked how its top managers did not know about this cheating, Horn replied, 'I agree. It's very hard to believe.'

If that were not enough, the world's largest companies have given the public many more offences to consider. In Brazil, oil giant Petrobras lost $2 billion – some paid in bribes and some illegally diverted into former executives' own bank accounts. Toshiba's past three presidents quit after the company was found to have inflated profits by $1.3 billion over seven years. And in the US, Turing Pharmaceuticals has been damned as 'morally clueless' after raising the price of a drug used to treat malaria in patients with weak immune systems by 5,000%.

Then there's FIFA, football's once-proud governing body, reduced to a shambolic mess when Sepp Blatter revealed that awarding the 2018 World Cup to Russia had been a fix, and admitted paying Michel Platini, president of UEFA, £1.3 million in a 'gentleman's agreement' over unspecified services. Blatter failed to embed in FIFA's culture its official rhetoric about acting for the good of the game and the global football family. FIFA's failings may have been spectacular, but they are not unique. Enron's official corporate values sounded good too: communication, respect, integrity and excellence.

Business has gone astray, losing touch with humanity by putting profit before principles and value before values. The pendulum has swung too far towards growth at any cost.

Focusing on values

In this post-coronavirus world, where so much needs to be rebuilt, business has the opportunity to seek to gain more trust from people by starting to actively solve some of the problems it has created. But changing cultures is not something that can be done overnight. It has to start with sustained, deep commitment from directors who know how to lead from the top.

An organisation must agree on what its values are, which is not as easy as it sounds. Too many companies think having an agreed set of values is unnecessary, taking instead the company line that 'people know what our values are because they are in the company's DNA'. And while many values might seem universal, the emphasis – and meaning – can vary from one organisation to another. Too many organisations act as if they can integrate ethics into their strategy by mere proclamation in the form of a 'mission statement'. Others turn to fashionable initiatives that, however well-intentioned, are doomed to fail if the foundations have not been laid.

When Google was listed on the New York Stock Exchange in 2004, its prospectus famously included the motto 'Don't be evil' and a resounding declaration that 'we will be better served – as shareholders and in all other ways – by a company that does good things for the world even if we forgo some short-term gains'.

Yet those words became an albatross for the technology giant when questions were asked about the way it tracked users across numerous devices with Google+, and the amount of tax it was not paying in the UK. Google UK's then chief, Matt Brittin, was hauled before the House of Commons Public Accounts Committee to be rebuked by Labour MP Margaret Hodge, who told him: 'I think that you do evil.' After such indignities, it was only a matter of time before the motto was changed. The rebranding of Google as Alphabet gave management the perfect opportunity to ditch the slogan, replacing it with the weaker 'Do the right thing'.

> What is the cost of lies? It's not that we will
> mistake them for the truth. The real danger
> is that if we hear enough lies then we won't
> recognise the truth at all. What will we do then?
> – HBO's MINISERIES CHERNOBYL

Business does not exist in isolation – it is part of a systemic matrix. We have reached a point where regulators, policy makers, the investor community, and finance, accounting and risk professions are waking up to the fact that having businesses that do not hold clear values and act accordingly is becoming unsustainable. Business ethics and behaviours are being brought to the fore, highlighting the fact that people and their behaviours are the biggest drivers of both value and risk in organisations.

The need for change in many corporate cultures is now more obvious than ever before. If we are to rebuild trust, we will have to understand and reform what drives the decisions that businesses make, embracing the triple bottom line, commonly termed the three Ps (people, planet, performance). Ex-Unilever CEO Paul Polman believes: 'Only organisations that state clearly what purpose they play in serving the community in which they operate, and align profit with that purpose, can contribute to societies in the long term.' Even though the company is listed on the New York and London stock exchanges, he went as far as scrapping quarterly reporting when he took the helm. Polman was open about the fact that Unilever's approach might not deliver the highest profitability every year, but he promised it would deliver consistently, year after year. And so it has. Stewardship does not manifest itself quarterly. A seed takes time to grow into a fruitful tree.

Incorporating personal ethics

Organisations need to think about how to create a long-term culture which increases the likelihood that people at every level of the organisation will make ethically sound decisions. Writing more rules or regulations is not the answer. Too many rules can work against individual understanding of accountability and ethics, demonstrated over many years through behavioural science. Nonetheless, command and control, manifested in endless policies and processes, remains a dominant mindset.

Ethics expert Roger Steare argues that it would be better if staff were encouraged to develop a 'moral DNA'. Employees can then evaluate their decisions, carefully and self-critically checking whether something feels right, and assessing the impact on stakeholders within the organisation, outside it and in the community at large. Values inspire people; mere rules squash such ethical engagement, and people look for ways around them. Besides, there can never be enough rules to cover all potential situations.

A set of values creates the framework within which staff can operate with flexibility and autonomy, while still remaining inside the ethical guidelines, which should ensure their actions are humane. It forces us to remind ourselves what it really means to live by and through an ethical value, to be a person of moral fibre. Values that are derived from an individual's ethical compass bring in the heart and the feeling functions, and an awareness about the impact of any action or policy on the wellbeing of others.

We all have a set of values through which we look at things. What we value guides not only our personal choices but also our perceptions of the worth of others. Values, therefore, become part of complex attitude sets that influence our behaviour and the behaviour of those with whom we interact.

When I was eighteen, I was offered a one-year contract at Walt Disney World in Florida for my 'gap year' between finishing school and starting university. I still remember our daily briefings there prior to going 'on show'. Our manager would say, 'This isn't rocket science. Go out there and create magic!' 'How?' we asked. However we pleased, as long as it was authentic and in line with the company's values.

Towards the end of my contract, I received a letter thanking me for changing someone's life. Initially, I could not recall the incident. As I read on, I remembered walking through the EPCOT park after a super-long shift one evening, and noticing a gentleman taking a photograph of a large group of people wearing the usual Mickey and Minnie ears. Exhausted, I might have walked past, but I had stopped to ask if I could take the photo for them before continuing on my way.

My heart sank when I read that the gentleman taking the photo had died in a car accident a week later – so I had captured the only photograph of him together with

his entire family. I was humbled to learn
that what was just a passing gesture to me
had been magical – and thus in line with
Disney's stated values – for someone else.

It makes sense of why Disney invested
so much in ensuring its recruitment process selected individuals whose personal
ethics were already clearly in place. And
Disney's own values were so deeply embedded that 'cast members' would constantly
search for ways to bring them to life.

A company's values cannot exist independently of the inherent
value systems of the individuals who work for it. Unless it hires only
those who are, so to speak, spontaneously ethical, it is unlikely that
a company which functions through rules alone will inspire and
convince its employees. If, as leaders, we want people to show up
with their humanity, we will need to empower employees to connect to the values congruently and authentically. If we allow for
some 'freedom within the frame', we will discover there is always
time for humanity.

Testing corporate values

Core values that are aligned with and embedded in an organisation
can be a source of competitive advantage, resulting in:

- A secure licence to operate
- A more engaged and autonomous workforce
- A more loyal and satisfied customer base

- Greater transparency
- Trust from stakeholders
- Stronger relationships with suppliers and partners in the value chain
- A more collaborative community
- A better ability to innovate

But announcing values and behaviours does not mean everyone will embrace them. Ron Carucci conducted a 15-year longitudinal study involving 3,200 interviews and 210 organisational assessments to see whether there were factors that predicted whether or not people inside a company would be honest. He discovered that when there is a lack of consistency between an organisation's stated mission, objectives and values, and the way they are actually experienced by employees and the marketplace, it is 2.83 times more likely to have people withhold or distort truthful information. When employees perceive duplicity between their organisation's stated identity and its actions, they eventually follow suit.

> I once arrived at a major hotel chain in Los Angeles, eager to pick up a parcel I had arranged to have delivered there. The receptionist told me she was unable to give me the parcel as the collection hours were from 12 noon to 2 p.m. only, and it was then 2.20 p.m. I explained that I could see the package just behind her – but to no avail. Rules were rules. The next day I went to collect the package, but it had gone missing (and was never

found). I wonder how the values of 'hospitality' and 'ownership' were being lived out in that company.

Empty values statements create cynical and dispirited employees, alienate customers and undermine managerial credibility. As leaders, we should ask ourselves, 'Do my people hide behind the rules, or stand in front of them?'

The cost of values

Coming up with strong values – and sticking to them – requires real guts. An organisation considering placing emphasis on its values must first come to terms with the fact that, when properly practised, values are a double-edged sword which can inflict pain on the one who wields it. They limit an organisation's strategic and operational freedom and constrain the behaviour of its people. They leave executives open to heavy criticism for even minor violations. And they demand constant vigilance. If leaders are not willing to accept the pain that real values can incur, they will be better off without them.

I recently travelled to the beautiful sultanate of Oman on business, and headed to the airport after a day of meetings. At check-in, a gentleman wearing an azure-blue-and-tan uniform and with an impressive moustache informed me that it would cost $30 to check in 'early'. I had arrived at his counter three hours and two minutes before departure, and check-in was free within three hours of departure. With no

Hermes
the parcel people

P1865520

- If you want to know what your parcel is up to, you can track it using the number above.
- If you've got a question about a return to a retailer, you'll need to contact them directly.
- Or, if you have any questions about any Hermes parcel, just visit our help section at **myhermes.co.uk**

Hermes

the parcel people

Receipt

Send, collect, return

This receipt is your proof of drop-off.

Date:

S/O

No. of parcels:

/

Thanks for using your local ParcelShop. Your parcel is in good hands.

other passengers around, we stared at each other like Ben Stiller's scene from *Meet the Parents*. One hundred and twenty seconds later he asked for my passport and I got the boarding card without charge. Once back home, I was relieved to find out that this particular airline has no espoused values, just images of their leadership team on the website in the usual serious-looking, black-and-white, side-on, arms-folded pose. In reality, values always exist; the question is whether they are intentional, accidental or hypocritical.

Embedding values

Values need to have a real, practical, everyday application in every part of the business, and values that are verbs are more easily actionable. If it is not clear what a particular value would mean both for someone in the customer service team and for someone in finance, then it is probably not one of the company's values.

If they are really going to take hold, core values need to be integrated into every employee-related process – hiring methods, performance management systems, criteria for promotions and rewards, even dismissal policies. Leadership and resilience capability should be developed in line with cultural and behavioural values. From the first interview to the last day of work, employees should be constantly reminded that core values form the basis for every decision the company makes. But beware that it is not used as a mechanism to perpetuate a lack of diversity by justifying hiring only those individuals who fit in with the majority and whose thinking aligns with the groupthink. The suitability of candidates should apply to alignment of values, not necessarily of thinking and experience, so that it becomes 'culture add' instead of 'culture fit'.

If taken seriously, such an embedding of values offers copious rewards.

In the mid-Noughties, Emirates held the intention of becoming the undisputed leader in airline service. At that time, Skytrax – the preeminent airline review and ranking site – was tracking them at number nine. Extensive internal and external research went into identifying the airline's 'service personality', at which point the building of a multi-million-dollar purpose-built facility was commissioned. If you ever travel to Dubai, look out for the famous aeroplane-shaped building. It houses five immersive learning zones for the airline's employees to get a very practical handle on the five values: personal, considerate, cosmopolitan, thorough and pioneering. To give some idea of the scale of the project, the venue houses a climbing wall (Mount Emirest!) with six means of ascent used to facilitate the visceral experience of what it is like to be a pioneer.

Every single member of staff went through the facilitated one-day experience, becoming conscious of what they were doing well, and what could be done even better, to go from good to great. Each zone focused on understanding the value, exploring the different ways to apply it, what worked best for each person and learning to adapt behaviour accordingly. Invitations were handwritten by the divisional president – there was even a video message from the ruler of Dubai. After all, Dubai needs Emirates, just as Emirates needs Dubai.

The experience was supported by a complete redesign of the employee deal, with leaders publishing their 'service personality promise' and getting feedback – by anyone at any time – on the extent to which they were living the values. Occasional moments of brilliance became more frequent as people shared stories of how it was coming to life in the workplace. My favourite has to be Mr Jones.

Mr Jones, a top-tier member of the airline's frequent traveller programme, was once very late boarding the plane from London Heathrow back to his home in Dubai. He finally appeared, running down the airbridge, shirt untucked and sweating profusely. After take-off, the flight purser respectfully approached him: 'Mr Jones, it's wonderful to have you back with us. I noticed something appeared to be the matter on boarding and wanted to know what I can do to help.' It turned out that Mr Jones had bargained with his seven-year-old daughter, Fifi, that he could miss her birthday because of his work on one condition – that he return with the latest Harry Potter book, unavailable in Dubai. In the kerfuffle of airport security at Heathrow, he had left her present in one of the screening trays. Unfortunately, nothing could be done to get that book back.

But the purser knew that a friend, an airport manager in Dubai, had recently returned from annual leave, and wondered if by any chance she might have brought any copies of the new book back with her. He sent a message to ground to find out. Six and a half hours later the flight landed, and the aircraft door opened. A hand reached around the door with a wrapped book and a card with a simple message: 'Here is the book, Mr Jones. We would hate for your daughter to be disappointed.'

Change journeys often take three to five years to become embedded. In 2013, Emirates was named World's Best Airline (and again in 2016) by Skytrax. The brand equity with being number one was worth billions.

Overcoming barriers to success

While change can come from anywhere, it is crucial that the founders and leadership team have bought into why values are important, so that they role-model the desired behaviours. It will not be enough to impose newly defined, explicit values simply by telling people what they are. The implicit, unwritten values of the current culture, and how these may be out of alignment with the new desired values and behaviours, will also need to be highlighted and articulated. Employee input and customer feedback can be very helpful in understanding these cultural issues and barriers.

Given the cynicism surrounding values in some quarters these days, leaders would do well to reiterate them whenever possible. It has been said that employees will not believe a message until they have heard it repeated by executives seven times. Leaders may wish to put values and culture on the standing agenda at executive committee and senior leadership team meetings, and ensure a specific board committee has oversight of conduct and culture.

It is not that employees see leaders as unethical per se, but they may very well see them as amoral – as possessing no meaningful vocabulary around values. And because behaviours are always contextual, the language used to describe the actions that support the value they represent should be appropriate for the context of the work unit. For example, the value of 'trust' on a factory floor may give more focus to competence-based behaviours, whereas 'trust' in a sales or accounting department may give more focus to character-based behaviours. National culture should also be taken into account. Where senior management is located in a foreign country, cultural differences may mean that the desired behaviours do not 'translate' into behaviours appropriate for the culture in question.

Being the best *for* the world

Aligning with meaningful values does not mean that a company inevitably stops growing and starts to lose money. Doing good in the world and making money are not mutually exclusive concepts. Indeed, the B Corporation movement has demonstrated the power of companies not just being the best *in* the world, but also the best *for* the world. Certified B Corporations are a new kind of business that balances purpose and profit. They are legally required to consider the impact of their decisions on workers, customers, suppliers, community and the environment. There are currently more than 3,000 Certified B Corporations in over 150 industries and 70 countries, with one unifying goal – to redefine success in business.

We have seen how short-termism can lead to aggressive, unethical cultures that promote growth at any cost. Business needs our humanity if we are to create healthy organisations that will be around for the long term. But values can only survive if we defend them actively. If some leaders choose to remain wilfully blind, and wonder whether all this is worth the effort, they would do well to remember that studies have consistently shown ethical companies perform better in the long term. And of course, by avoiding a scandal on their watch, they could be saving a multi-billion-dollar write-down – and their jobs.

In our quest to better understand the obstacles to more ethical working practices, it is now time to go beneath the water line and examine culture – this mysterious thing 'hidden in plain sight' that is all around us. It drives our behaviour, impacts almost everything that happens in our teams and organisations, and yet we can rarely define it, and are seldom fully aware of it.

Culture Shift

Culture is to humans what water is to fish.
It is the water we swim in every day.
– DAVID FOSTER WALLACE

n 2005, David Foster Wallace addressed the graduating class at Kenyon College. He began with a parable:

There are these two young fish swimming along and they happen to meet an older fish swimming the other way, who nods at them and says, 'Morning, boys. How's the water?' The two young fish swim on for a bit, and then eventually one of them looks over at the other and goes, 'What the hell is water?'

Defining culture
Culture
n: The shared values, norms and expectations that govern the way people approach their work and interact with each other.

Organisational culture may be defined as a set of 'shared mental assumptions' that guide behaviours in the workplace.

Climate
n: The sense, feeling or atmosphere people experience in an organisation.

If culture refers to 'the way we do things around here', climate refers to the feel of the environment, i.e. employee engagement.

Norms
n: Written and unwritten rules about how people should behave in a system.

Norms affect our cultural identity. They are the informal rules, expectations and understandings that guide the behaviour in any given situation.

A source of competitive advantage

From the moment an organisation has more than one employee, it begins to nurture a set of shared behaviours that define how people work together. Culture is built through shared learning and experience. It usually happens by default – not design – evolving as sales gain traction in the marketplace.

Leaders gravitate to what they are incentivised to do, and therefore spend more time and energy on products and services than on culture. Nonetheless, culture is a genuine source of competitive advantage in today's economy. The ability to have employees bring their full energy, intellect, passion, curiosity and desire to participate in an organisation is the ultimate business impact.

As the late Herb Kelleher said of his airline, Southwest Airlines, 'Competitors can buy tangible assets, but they can't buy culture.' The airline prides itself on not taking itself too seriously (check out their famous safety demonstration rap on YouTube). Indeed, Herb was certainly the only company president I know of who would turn up at aircraft maintenance hangars at 2 a.m. wearing a flowered hat, feather boa and a purple dress to reinforce Southwest's one-of-a-kind culture. An excerpt from the company website states:

> *Our culture is often imitated, and never duplicated. Every employee is responsible for promoting and preserving our*

culture. We also have a culture services department that is charged with championing a culture through which every employee knows he or she matters.

Our culture is woven into all aspects of our business and our employees' lives, from the way employees treat each other to the way that our company puts our employees first. Three vital elements of our culture are appreciation, recognition, and celebration.

In order to promote and foster a fun and healthy work environment, we work to appreciate every employee through local and company-wide culture committees.

The word 'culture' remains one of the most widely used – but least understood – words in the business lexicon (the Merriam-Webster dictionary declared it the word of the year for 2014). The vast majority of what you hear about culture is actually focused on the business environment. Most 'culture surveys' and diagnostics only measure aspects of the organisational climate.

Climate is very important, but it gives lag indicators, a way of looking backward and determining the big picture of how leaders have done. It is an overall measure of past performance, similar to driving with your focus on the rear-view mirror. It includes employee pulse/satisfaction surveys, football tables and free food or Friday drinks in the office. If climate is like weather (the environment) – how things are showing up – then culture is the meteorology that produces the weather. It is much deeper, providing leading indicators that predict future success. Like focusing attention on the windshield, it tells leaders how they are driving towards a goal that lies ahead. Gaining an understanding of the underlying culture is critical for accelerating change efforts and delivering sustainable results.

Culture is the assumptions, beliefs and expectations for behaviour established through organisational structures, systems, technologies, communication processes and leadership practices. According to Professor Edgar Schein, there are three levels of culture – artefacts (what is observable), values (what is stated) and underlying assumptions (not stated anywhere but people instinctively follow). Most leaders focus too much on artefacts or values and fail to examine the underlying assumptions.

Unspoken rules

Culture drives everything that happens in an organisation, whether spoken or unspoken. After graduation, I went to work for a major international airline. As an #avgeek, I had written to that airline when I was 11 years old to say, 'One day I will work for you.' They replied, 'See you in ten years!' It was a very proud moment for me when that letter was read out at my leadership graduation ceremony 15 years later, as I became the youngest flight purser in the company's history.

It was my bad luck (fate) to come into contact with a disgruntled first officer on a particular flight to Paris. During the pre-flight briefing, the pilots came to speak to us for a couple of minutes (there was a 65-inch screen at the back of the room

with a countdown for when we had to depart).
In the briefing, the first officer proclaimed, 'No phones and cameras allowed,'
but as he spoke with a strong accent, I did
not catch his words. I put my hand up to ask
for clarification (if you want hierarchical
systems, work in aviation), but the pilots
had already walked off. Fast-forward ten
minutes and we were in the crew bus heading
towards the aircraft stand. I was chatting
to the Seychellois crew member sitting next
to me when I remembered that I needed to
switch off my old Nokia phone.

Seeing me grab my phone out of my bag,
the first officer screamed, 'STOP!' Cabin
bags flew forward, and the crew's screams
reverberated until we came to a halt. The
first officer proceeded, 'We will continue
when THIS guy gets off his phone.' It
took me a few moments to realise he was
addressing me – in front of the 26 crew,
from 26 nations, whom I was meant to be
leading to deliver the finest, safest in-
flight experience. We reached the aircraft
stand a few minutes later. I got off the
bus and asked to speak to the first officer, in the hope of explaining what I had
actually been doing. Not only was I not
heard, but I was treated to some exotic
language before being headbutted and left
on the tarmac, injured and embarrassed.

I and several other crew members reported the incident to the most senior folks in In-Flight Services, but I heard nothing more. Several months later, as I was checking in at the crew briefing centre for a 17-hour flight to Houston, I was approached by someone in management. The person tilted her head, lowered her gaze to my name badge and said, 'It's Samie, isn't it? Samie, we know what happened to you was wrong. But in aviation, pilots are considered more powerful than cabin crew. I need you to drop this, otherwise it could create some waves, and we wouldn't want anyone to drown, would we?' Not only did I drop it, but I had to admit my lack of insistence on understanding the first officer's proclamation in the briefing room had been the genesis of the incident.

That incident was perhaps the best culture lesson I could have asked for in preparation for my imminent transition into a career in banking. That day I learnt that I was subjected to invisible power structures that would excuse almost any behaviour from the privileged few. I would soon discover that financial services institutions set aside billions each year to pay for values breaches caused by the imperatives of their culture. The cost of doing business.

Blind spots

Have you ever worked for a company that rewards fitting in over being extraordinary? The blind spot here could be 'Playing by the rules matters more than the customer' or 'Bosses reward mediocre employees and fear top performers'.

Perhaps you have been blamed for something at work that was not your fault. Did it leave you ostracised by your work colleagues? Scapegoating is inevitable in a climate that venerates business leaders as heroes. If organisational leaders are framed as heroic, then they have to have villains to slay or scapegoats to malign. It is part of the narrative.

As leaders, if we are to know what to preserve and what to change, then it is critical to understand the underlying assumptions that hold the culture together. Cultural blind spots are the information embedded within our behaviour and practices that we take for granted and typically overlook when paying attention elsewhere. They are part of an area that cannot be directly observed under existing circumstances. We thus risk neglecting them and their significance. All people and organisations have blind spots – even the best of us. To illuminate them, we must slow down and examine the things that are present but not always seen, which is exactly what you are doing by reading this book.

Blind spots create unwritten ground rules. If a person goes out of their way to help a colleague and no one recognises that extra effort, then an unwritten rule might be 'Around here, it's not worth your while to help others out'. If a boss says, 'In this organisation, we care for our people', and then treats someone without respect, an unspoken rule becomes 'Management here says one thing and means another'. Actions really do speak louder than words – who gets hired, fired and promoted is a more powerful indicator than any written rules.

Some executives go 'undercover' to learn exactly what it is like to work on the front line, and in so doing uncover blind spots in the system. Others, like those at Disney, go on planned rotation across various roles, which gives a first-hand depth of understanding, from which creativity and empathy arise. Using these feedback channels, leaders quickly learn what is aligned with their desired culture and what is not. Only with an honest understanding of relationships, norms and practices can leaders be confident they are leading the business in such a way that the culture – and their employees – can thrive.

Digging deeper into culture

While it is seductive to focus on the behaviour, in the early stages the emphasis needs to be on the overarching reinforcement systems, processes and procedures driving that behaviour. Culture is also about the systems, structures and processes that have led people to believe they should behave in certain ways.

Some years ago, I was brought in to assist a government authority that wanted to bring its values to life and evolve its culture. It soon transpired that the systems and processes of other government entities were getting in the way, and we were in danger of losing momentum as workers tried to bring the desired cultural attributes to life, but were met with blockages from various forces elsewhere in the larger system. Culture is like the organisation's immune system, and will send antibodies to prevent change. I recommend doing a 'pre-mortem' beforehand to identify as many things as possible that could kill it.

Back in 2013, I worked with a bank in the Sultanate of Oman to support their leaders with a cultural integration programme for a merger. A Western bank with five branches in Oman merged with a local bank with ninety branches, each operating to very different standards and in different languages. Bringing the two together was, therefore, an intricate task, at both a practical and cultural level.

The Sultanate of Oman is geographically complex – bordered by Yemen and situated very close to Iran – with a significant segment of customers having no fixed address. Some branches were in extremely remote locations, making it difficult to visit them all in person.

There was a great deal of pride in local banks from their employees and citizens, which needed to be acknowledged and honoured in the new entity. We spoke to them extensively before placing culture (how we operate) between purpose (why we exist) and strategy (what we do). Once we had established the 'tone from the top', we turned our attention to the 'tone from above'.

We introduced a structure of regional managers and coaches who played an integral

role in embedding the culture and promoting values to employees on the front
line. Group programmes did not cut the
mustard, so we invested in bespoke micro-
learning solutions that were tailored for
our audience and would allow employees to
absorb them quickly. Middle managers were
developed to take responsibility for reinforcing and embedding learning outcomes
in their area, so that learning became
employee-owned and manager-supported.

We named the long adventure we embarked
upon *Our Journey to Success*. By 2017 the
bank had been named 'Best Bank in Oman' by
Euromoney.

Implementing culture change

Lasting change requires the unwavering commitment of the top team – who will have the biggest stakes in terms of letting go of status, entitlement and perceived power. CEOs and chairpersons who give only lip service to a transformation will find others doing the same. Only the boss of all bosses can ensure that the right people spend the right amount of time driving the necessary changes.

A change management process is essential for developing and implementing a plan, but leaders who want to shift cultures should not allow the process to overshadow the 'human touch'. People will willingly support it when they are involved and it touches them at the deepest level of their feelings, emotions and thinking.

As such, it is worth remembering that successful solutions are based on the principle that resolution occurs by fostering the positive, and not attacking the negative. Socrates wisely commented that the secret of change is to focus energy not on fighting the old but on building the new.

Culture change lives in the collective hearts and habits of people and their shared perception of 'how things are done around here'. Someone with authority can demand compliance, but they cannot dictate the optimism, trust, conviction or creativity needed to inculcate real change. True commitment requires going beneath the water line to work with belief systems.

Shifting beliefs

Change is most likely to last when it is built on a foundation of supportive new experiences and the resulting newly fashioned beliefs.

Most leaders focus on the actions that need to be performed in order to implement a change. But the pathway to achieving sustainable culture change involves first identifying the kind of experiences a team needs in order to leave the old ways behind and fully support the new approach. These experiences will influence the beliefs of the employees to further support that change. At this point, new actions can be created to move towards the desired goal. In order to shift to a new way of doing things, we need a new set of experiences, beliefs and actions to get us there. After all, people have to experience something before they can believe in it.

Take a weight-loss journey or health goal as an example. After making New Year's resolutions, most of our focus goes on the actions ('I need to go to the gym to get fit'). What we do not always look at are the beliefs we hold about the changes we want to make ('but I feel judged by the gym bunnies'). If we have had bad experiences at the gym – and from them we have come to believe that exercising there is not our thing – it will be very difficult to lose weight, unless we look for a different experience with different beliefs attached to it in order to embrace the new actions we want to be successful. In my case, I invited some friends to join me at the gym. The experience of having that community of support helped shift my beliefs around self-confidence. We motivated each other – and held one another accountable for sticking to our fitness plans, thereby achieving our goals.

I worked with a client in their manufacturing division to get to zero safety incidents by embedding their organisational values and evolving the culture. If we focused solely on changing actions, it would have sounded like 'don't text while walking, hold on to the handrail, use the zebra crossing when crossing the facility, put on your personal protective equipment'. In that scenario, it is likely that the leader would need to be around to ensure compliance.

One definition of culture is 'what you do when no one is watching'. Therefore, we worked with the client to create new experiences around leaders sharing their personal stories from other sites, spending more time coaching, making it a positive thing to raise 'unsafe conditions', using gamification (the application of game-design elements and principles in non-game contexts) to bring the tools and techniques to life. Over time, the beliefs in the system started to shift – 'perhaps the leaders really mean it, perhaps they do care, safety is a choice, it is not us against them, we should all place equal onus on getting to the target of zero safety incidents'. Creating a proactive and consistent safety-first culture led to better-protected people, improved operational performance and reduced downtime. Over the course of 18 months, the company moved to the first quartile (top 25th percentile) for safety performance according to the manufacturing classification's total recordable incident rate (TRIR).

The importance of communication

On the change journey, transparency is key. In the absence of information, rumours and frustration will fill the void. Lean towards over-communicating. When facts are scarce, dispel rumours and share what is known, as I am sure you did when leading remote teams during the COVID-19 crisis.

Think about times you have been kept on hold on the telephone without the agent coming back to you. I have worked with pilots who communicated regularly during a delay – even if it was bad news, passengers appreciated the transparent and regular updates. I have also worked with pilots who were busy fixing the problem and did not update passengers on the progress. These usually ended up being the flights from hell.

As the company's transformation progresses, a powerful way to reinforce the story is to spotlight the successes. Stories are a universal cultural language that can be used to provide context and meaning.

Princeton University neuroscientist and researcher Uri Hasson has shown that brainwaves start to oscillate together between the storyteller and listeners, with blood flowing to the same regions of the brain, in what he describes as 'brain alignment'. If we want people to bring their humanity – or curiosity, empathy, vulnerability – to work, we might share a story about when we realised its importance for us personally. It will be as though they are sharing in the same experience.

Movement makers are also very good at recognising the power of celebrating small wins. Research has shown that demonstrating efficacy is one way that movements bring in people who are sympathetic but not yet mobilised to join. People will go to extraordinary lengths for causes they believe in, and a powerful transformation story will create and reinforce their commitment.

Measuring the impact

While measuring culture is a challenging task, it is also a necessity. To maintain a healthy culture, management needs to be able to observe and track behaviour through meaningful metrics. These should be analysed as a trend rather than a single number or point in time. In addition, the analysis should look not just at individual metrics in isolation but at how the data interacts.

Creating a dashboard that uses both efficiency and effectiveness metrics against baseline indicators will help to demonstrate the shift from current to target state and the impact on business outcomes. A range of qualitative and quantitative measures and proxy indicators across the business, employee lifecycle and customer journey is essential. Also important is that social and eco responsibility are captured, and that both leading and lagging metrics are used: the forward-looking metrics are key to identifying what might happen rather than only reporting on what did happen. The reporting tool should be flexible, providing multiple views and the types of metrics needed to meet the needs of multiple audiences.

Ensuring lasting change

Shifting cultures should not be approached as a project or an initiative – it should be regarded as an ongoing process of values management that becomes deeply engrained into the ethos of the organisation. It is better to avoid using terminology like 'training' or 'programme', otherwise employees could see it as 'flavour of the month' or another box to tick. I worked with a client in Asia to put measures around the extent that new values-aligned behaviours were being demonstrated in the organisation. The uptake was significant until the site goal was achieved, at which point the line in the graph dipped off. In other words, the values themselves had become another key performance indicator (KPI).

Remember, organisations do not transform. People do. By creating corporate cultures that align with mainstream societal needs and values, we start to break down the barriers between people's home and professional lives. And if we go back to one of the origins of the word 'culture', we get 'cultura' – the cultivation of the soul. This makes sense to me. We are working with the soul, the root, the vulnerabilities and strengths of both business and individual – both searching for meaning, a reason for being, in today's world. One feeds the other. The person feeds the organisation as the organisation feeds the person. And both must be awake and conscious of this relationship for it to thrive. But as we will discover, the traditional notion of success is designed to keep us asleep.

The Talent Trip

Everybody is talented because everybody
who is human has something to express.
– BRENDA UELAND

Success the old way

Imagine finding the editor-in-chief of the *Huffington Post* lying
unconscious on the floor of her office in a pool of her own blood.
That's exactly what happened on the morning of 6th April 2007
when Arianna Huffington's head hit the corner of her desk, resulting in a cut eye and a broken cheekbone. She had collapsed due to
exhaustion and lack of sleep. As she waited in the emergency room,
she asked herself, 'Is this really success?'

Success is traditionally defined by two things: money and power.
Many still believe that working 24/7 is the way to success – to work
beyond our limits, to sleep less and do more. Arianna saw around
her a society in which success is equated with exhaustion. Successful
people are supposed to devote themselves completely to their profession, pulling all-nighters, sacrificing weekends, families and happiness. We plug ourselves in, but never unplug. Our work has come to

dominate everything, as if that defines us. We plan our day around recharging our devices, but rarely do the same with ourselves. We take better care of our smartphones than we do of ourselves.

And by acting this way, some people achieve wealth and power. But does that really make them successful? We only have around 30,000 days – that is 1,000 months to play the game of life, of which 400 months are spent queuing and sleeping. If you have been to a memorial lately, you will have noticed that eulogies have very little to do with our LinkedIn profiles.

Our egos would have us believe that the more we do, the more we become. This idea of success can work – or at least appear to work – in the short term. But over the long term, power and money by themselves are like a two-legged stool – we can balance on them for a while, but eventually we will topple over. The path of forced effort and struggle ultimately limits our success because it is based on the ego's insecurities and struggles for power, approval and safety.

I work out by indoor cycling, often called spinning – a fitness class featuring adapted exercise bikes and a 'power board' on which each rider's statistics are displayed, with those whose scores are highest gaining special recognition. In a typical class the instructor leads riders through routines simulating hill climbs, sprints and interval training, but there is no compulsion to follow the suggested sequence, and riders primarily motivated by dominating the scoreboard tend to do their own thing, focusing on sprinting to maximise points. Occasionally the screen is not functioning, and I have noticed that in these sessions, everyone seems to follow the instructor's programme. No judgements here; simply an observation that some of us seem to be motivated by the 'what' (points) more than the 'how' (the way the points are achieved) in many facets of our life. Hardly surprising, given society's obsession with status, numbers and results.

Understanding the messages of our biology

So, if this is how we behave even outside of work, what might lie behind it? Could there be a physiological advantage to acting this way?

Inside us we have a quartet of chemicals that are primarily responsible for our happiness:

- **Serotonin** provides the feeling of significance, pride and status. It flows when we feel important and drives us to seek the recognition of others. 'I want to do it for my parents, my boss, my partner.' It reinforces the sense of allegiance, of relationships with the group.
- **Dopamine** motivates us to achieve incremental goals and rewards-motivated behaviour. It makes us feel good when we check things off the 'to do list' or get through project milestones.
- **Oxytocin** creates intimacy and trust and strengthens relationships. Mothers, babies and partners feel this when they are giving and receiving protection and love.
- **Endorphins** are released in response to pain and stress, and help to alleviate anxiety. They keep us going during workouts and give us a 'runner's high', good for those late nights and 70+ hour weeks.

According to Simon Sinek, a healthy corporate culture is one where the four chemicals are operating in balance with each other. Individuals are energised by endorphins and motivated by dopamine, and teams come together through a sense of pride (serotonin) and creating connections for the common good (oxytocin). However, these biologically fuelled motivators do not always have a positive impact on the working environment, leading to further distortion in the measurement of success in the workplace.

Dopamine, in particular, has a highly addictive quality, and is also released by alcohol, nicotine and gambling. In toxic corporate cultures, we can get addicted to performance and ignore the rules. In such instances, there is also an increase in cortisol (stress, anxiety), which inhibits oxytocin, and thereby reduces our capacity for empathy, connection and trust.

Rewarding the wrong way

It seems our biology has not always helped us when it comes to our working culture, and that we would do well to be more aware of its hidden effects. Money, for example, carries an 'emotional charge' that goes far beyond its economic function. It is a tool we can use to acquire things we desire, which means we covet it, but compelling neuroscientific experiments show that it also acts like a drug, stimulating areas of the brain associated with immediate gratification through the release of dopamine.

I was preparing to speak at a large corporate event when a senior leader from the business approached me and said, 'I want to warn you, Samie. Pay letters went out yesterday, so some people might be very disengaged.' It got me thinking: pay is meant to motivate employees and improve performance, but does it actually do so?

A better understanding of the psychology of pay could end our fixation with annual increases and performance-related bonuses. 'Psychological research has consistently suggested that where money has motivational power it is nearly always negative,' writes Adrian Furnham, professor of psychology at University College, London in *The New Psychology of Money*. A major reason is that money (an extrinsic reward) crowds out our innate desire to do a good job (intrinsic reward) and leads to behaviours that work against employers' interests.

This emotional charge of money manifests even in very simple experiments that show people are drawn to the physical form of money: we feel a sense of loss when a familiar coin changes shape, even though its value remains the same. We manage virtual money less effectively than cash (worrying, as we are increasingly forced to move to a cashless society). Moreover, money is symbolic. Pay is a form of social approval. The obvious inference is that if organisations want to motivate their staff, they should decouple pay from performance and introduce incentives that play to humanity's intrinsic motivations, which are generally agreed to be autonomy (the ability to direct your own life and work), mastery (the opportunity to get better at something that matters) and purpose (the desire to do what we do in service of something larger than ourselves).

Would performance fall as a result? Dan Ariely conducted an experiment, asking groups of volunteers to repeatedly drag a circle on a computer screen into a box and recording how many times they did it in five minutes. He paid the first group $5 for their efforts, the second group 50 cents and the third group nothing – but told them they would be doing him a favour. The first group dragged on average 159 circles into the box, the second group dragged 101 circles and the third, 168. This, says Ariely, demonstrates that incentive pay can work in certain circumstances, to a certain extent. The fact that the most productive group was the one doing a favour illustrates the supremacy of social norms over market norms – of values over value.

Another lesson from behavioural science is that people react more strongly to something being withdrawn, even if they do not particularly value it, than they do to something being given to them, even if the new thing is of higher value. In psychological terms, this is known as 'loss aversion'. In short, you can lose £5 one day and find £5 the next, but you will not feel as if you have broken even.

According to behavioural scientists, performance-related pay fails on several counts. It undermines our need for autonomy (because of the monitoring required); it works against our innate desire for fairness if we see others earning more; and if we get a smaller proportion of performance-related pay one year, we suffer from loss aversion.

There are insights to be gained from the growing body of research that can give reward practitioners a better understanding of how to incentivise people at all levels. It will require a cultural shift from traditional extrinsic motivators, like annual bonuses and long-term incentive plans, towards intrinsic motivators.

Incidentally, you can get as much dopamine from someone saying 'thank you' or 'well done' as you can from getting a pay rise. The chemical effect is the same.

The trouble with 'talent'

Of course, we have to deliver performance at work. The point is that it is unbalanced when the predominant means by which we reward and recognise is by numbers. This is where 'talent' comes in – the people whom Arianna Huffington described as often sacrificing the most in order to be seen (validated) by management because they are deemed to drive the most value. But *do* they?

In her TED Talk, *Why It's Time to Forget the Pecking Order at Work*, Margaret Heffernan explains how many companies are run according to 'the super-chicken model', where the value is placed on star employees who outperform others. Using this model, scientists at Purdue University set out to build a flock of successful chickens by selectively breeding the best of the flock.

What should have amounted to a breed of 'super chickens' turned out to be a lesson about the world around us. The 'super chicken' flock ended up with only three living birds – the unfortunate result of the chickens killing each other off – while the original, 'average' flock ended up thriving, plump and healthy. It turned out that the success of the 'super chickens' was only achieved by eliminating the competition, and not by working together – that was the flock's downfall.

Of the many times I have failed (spectacularly) in my career, I got one of my most valuable lessons at a five-star hotel in London. I was asked by a client to do 'something special' for the talent cohort. I was in the process of deploying a values and culture change experience for senior leaders across the group, and I colluded with the client by organising to run two cohorts on the same day – one for talent and one for…well, the others. The 'special ones' got dinner the night before, along with networking opportunities with highfalutin people. We had planned to make this cohort the 'culture champions' or 'ambassadors' to leverage their potential and maximise the impact.

I was leading the facilitation of the 'others'. In the course of the day there was laughter and tears, and people spoke up. We tackled some of the most challenging issues in the system and found a way to align meaningfully around the values and purpose of the organisation.

Next door was a different story. There was hardly a peep from the room all day. For sure, everyone 'looked' engaged, but the session lacked depth. It was then I came to realise that talent has more to lose. And what is the best way to fit in and look good? Avoid confrontation so as not to rock the boat. Toeing the company line and playing politics to gain influence is a sure way to keep your head. As I once heard a banker say, 'No one ever got sacked for saying "yes" to things. You get sacked for saying "no".'

Speaking up is a cornerstone for building an open and accountable workplace culture. Some companies canvass feedback from employees and then classify those who challenge the status quo as 'negative'. I was working with a client in Europe who wanted to implement a radical new system for organisational governance. Excitement was high, but understanding low. In a functional meeting one of the team exclaimed, 'There is so much more we have to think about before we agree to supporting the business with this.' The chief HR officer apologised to me afterwards for the individual's negativity. I had a different perspective – I was grateful that someone had had the courage to speak up. We should be worried when the most passionate people become quiet.

I have always been uncomfortable with the term 'talent'. A few weeks prior to the COVID-19 pandemic, supermarket workers, delivery drivers, social workers, garbage collectors and cleaners were considered low-skilled workers and accorded very little status or importance. But the changing circumstances quickly altered the perceived value of such occupations. Suddenly faced with the looming prospect of unemployment, 36,000 Australians applied for 5,000 shelf-stacking jobs at Coles supermarket in just 48 hours. A reminder that talent should think twice before valuing itself more highly than other social roles, however humble they may be. We are much more than the economy says we are.

Too old for talent?

You will find that most talent programmes are inherently ageist. Talk of 'high potentials' is often shorthand for 'young'. Though older employees can be included in such initiatives, the concept lends itself to those who have recently joined an organisation, and who exhibit the ambition and willingness to advance quickly. The jargon – whether 'fast track', 'high potential' or 'high flier' – only exacerbates the problem. And in this way, language becomes part of the stories we tell ourselves to justify the biases we create.

The Chartered Institute of Personnel and Development's (CIPD) *People Management* publication has revealed a growing body of academic and anecdotal evidence that suggests over-50s face deeply unfair barriers in the recruitment process, despite corporate commitments to diversity and inclusion. Too few companies audit their age profile in the same way they do gender or ethnicity. Career sites and company brochures often portray teams of young people, something that can put off older employees from applying for a role, even if their skills and experience are a perfect match. Although it is recommended that age be removed from CVs, the topic often comes up at the interview phase in any case.

The UK's demographics are such that the fastest-growing segment of the workforce is the over-50s. Increasing life expectancy will inevitably lead to the extension of our working lives. For the first time, the proportion of UK employees working beyond what used to be retirement age is growing more quickly than the numbers entering work.

Research shows that an age-diverse workforce pays dividends in much the same way as gender and ethnic diversity do, by enabling organisations to better understand and meet the needs of their diverse customer base. Employers need to get to grips with how to manage the varying needs of a workforce that spans multiple generations. This means thinking carefully about the way jobs are designed, how to attract, recruit and retain talent, and how to train managers to effectively manage older as well as younger workers. It also calls for new approaches to learning and knowledge-sharing, reflecting the different stages of people's careers, and seeking to ensure that all of humanity has the opportunity for fulfilling, productive work.

Changing work spaces and work forces

When we change the way we see the world, it influences what we do as well as the results we obtain. We now realise there is a different way to attract talent and drive performance.

Leaders in the United Arab Emirates (UAE) knew this when they endeavoured to create a more diversified knowledge-based economy that was less reliant on petrochemicals. Instead of simply buying planes from original equipment manufacturers (OEMs) like Airbus and Boeing, they wanted to develop their own engineering capabilities in this sector to become a single-source Tier 1 supplier to the aviation market. To do this, they founded Strata Manufacturing in 2009.

The mandate was to attract and develop a workforce, comprising 50% national citizens, to build advanced composite aerostructures, without any history of manufacturing capability in the country. Before arriving on the scene, I had been told it was a green-field project. It looked more like a yellow-sand one – there was literally nothing there except a derelict Russian cargo jet resting on one wingtip among sand dunes stretching as far as the eye could see.

The company was located in the remote town of Al Ain, most of whose male inhabitants travelled to Abu Dhabi or Dubai for work, leaving the women behind with barely any employment opportunities. We probably could have made a case for throwing lots of money at it, doubling salaries to entice the men to stay and work in Al Ain, as well as flying in foreign talent. Instead we took the bold move of engaging the local community to see if we could evolve together. We switched our focus to women, most of whom had never worked before and did not speak English.

We embarked on language classes, while simultaneously partnering with the OEMs on knowledge transfer. We collaborated with universities and colleges to adopt aeronautical and aerospace manufacturing degrees. We even partnered with KidZania, the educational theme park for children, to create manufacturing parks and programmes that could be used to inspire future generations to consider a career that was previously taboo.

When they spoke enough English, each technician was issued with a logbook and started recording every hour under expert supervision to reach the 2,000+ hours required for certification. Clearly defined career development pathways were mapped out for each employee, depending on personal situation and career aspirations.

Today, 58% of Strata's employees are Emirati nationals, of whom nearly 90% are women. Most of these are now classified as highly skilled workers and are directly involved in manufacturing operations. It is quite wonderful to see empowered women, wearing their national dress adjusted for safety, building aeroplane parts in a 24-hour facility in the desert.

Paving the way for a new kind of leadership?

Younger generations are not so interested in pursuing careers that will take them down the path of money and power. There is a discernible shift towards the values of self-expression, collective creativity, inclusiveness and authenticity. The ubiquitous question for Gen Y is not 'What do you do?' but 'Why do you do it?'.

Millennials and post-millennials will explore new solutions even if they are perceived as controversial. They will bring new energy to business, government and education, and will fight for change, even if it requires them to be more direct and less diplomatic. Collaboration will be in their DNA, and inspiration their measure of success.

Back to my cycle spinning class. I used to have a tendency to hide in a corner at the back of the room. One of the instructors would joke on the microphone, 'There's no hiding from me.' But another one said, 'I see you, Samie.' It is the same role, almost the same concept, but two different attitudes. Invariably, the latter improved my performance, especially when the instructor added, 'And I'm right there with you.'

The second instructor was working from a new paradigm, in which it is not all about competition to drive people – it is about understanding that cooperation and connection support people better. She knew that inclusiveness and validation get better results, which is surely what all leaders are striving to do. Talent, in and of itself, validates only a few. It turns out, the antidote is conscious leadership.

Part Two – The Awakening Present

Conscious Leadership in a Global World

The world is changed by your
example, not by your opinion.
— PAULO COELHO

The essence of leadership has always been about sensing and actualising the future. The Indo-European root of the English word leadership is 'leith', which means 'to go forth' and 'to cross a threshold'. It is about crossing the threshold and stepping into a new territory, into a future that is different from the past. One that brings the world together in a new form of global leadership.

Entering the age of the conscious leader

Raj Sisodia, professor of global business at Babson College, has done extensive research on how to create ethical and sustainable organisations. His research has shown that the most successful organisations are those 'not with your traditional hired gun-type CEOs who manage by the numbers and are driven by the bottom-line, where everything is seen through the lens of economic value'. They are the ones with individuals who are passionate about the purpose of the business. Sisodia describes these as 'conscious leaders', whose success rests on traits such as 'the capacity for love and care', alongside 'high levels of spiritual, systems and emotional intelligence'.

In its simplest form, conscious leadership refers to the ability to bring one's entire self into the position. Conscious leaders do not focus only on themselves, but instead on the entire system as a whole. Indeed, the English word 'conscious' is derived from the Latin *conscius* (*con* 'together' and *scio* 'to know').

Of course, there are also the microcosmic aspects of a holistic approach to bear in mind. Being a leader in today's world requires much more than operating skills, technical understanding and financial knowledge. To thrive in the 21st century, we need to enable people with the skills and character to lead effectively through the complexities of this era.

The first global leaders

Historically, multi-national organisations sent their talent from group headquarters to lead regional and local units. It was a rare foreign national who made it to the decision-making headquarters of these multi-national organisations, much less ascended to the top of the corporation.

All too often these expatriate leaders saw their mission as transferring headquarters' standards, processes, control systems and marketing approaches into their new locality. Such a model often meant that they failed to take advantage of the creative skills of their local teams and lacked the ability to translate global strategies into meeting the needs of local markets.

But the days of a dominant language and national culture within large international organisations are fading rapidly. The Western narrative is not enough. Siemens' ex-CEO Peter Löscher said in a 2008 interview, 'Siemens is not achieving its full potential on the international stage because its management is too white, too German and too male. We are too one-dimensional.'

Demographic trends indicate that in the second half of the 21st century, most of the workforce will be non-Western, non-white, non-male. Global intelligence – or GQ as Harvard Business School professor Bill George puts it – is the next frontier. It will require a new leadership language that is inclusive of all of humanity, as opposed to the speech without substance or content that we have become accustomed to in meetings ('let's square the circle, take it offline, put in place the building blocks, set the direction of travel, find the difference that makes a difference, dial up the volume...').

There are over 195 nations on earth, 6,500 spoken languages and 65 million refugees. Conscious leadership requires mastery in cultural and global intelligence, which we currently just do not possess.

> Not the ones speaking the same
> language, but the ones sharing the same
> feeling understand each other.
> – RUMI

Small things that big leaders may not know

Everyone knows that Arabs do not eat pork, but is everyone aware that it is bad manners to point one's foot at an Arab during conversation? Do not openly admire their possessions either, as they may feel obliged to give them to you.

Did you know that in some European countries sending yellow flowers to a woman signifies that she has been unfaithful to her husband? Or that you should not open gifts in front of Asians and Arabs when an exchange of presents is taking place? In Asia, one generally wraps up presents in red paper, while white is an unlucky colour, associated with death. On the other hand, avoid signing your name in red in the East, as it represents death in some Asian countries.

French and Hispanic people indulge in the nose twitch, snort or sniff to express alertness, disapproval or disdain respectively. The Portuguese tug their earlobes to indicate tasty food, though this gesture has sexual connotations in Italy. In Spain the same action means someone is not paying for their drinks, and in Malta it signifies an informer.

As leaders and agents of change, we need to deepen our understanding of the global village we operate in, and be flexible in our style and approach. If we cannot use hierarchy to change the system, then the main leverage we have is the quality of our relationship with other stakeholders. Jim Rohn used to say we are the product of the five people we most associate with. This means that our innermost circle plays a huge role in our personal character. Conscious leadership, therefore, requires us to escape the echo chambers of towns, cities, our preferred news channel and social media platform in order to expand our worldview.

The world needs leaders to have more of an understanding of how national culture intersects with organisational culture. We are used to having a code for behaviour taught by parents and teachers, and confirmed by peers and contemporaries. When someone begins to formulate an international code for behaviour, they instinctively look to their own norms as being the logical, acceptable, inoffensive ones. But that approach can only get us so far. All over the world thousands of misunderstandings are caused every day through such simple mistakes.

In his book *When Cultures Collide*, Richard D. Lewis offers us some light-hearted and not overly damaging examples:

Germany

- What is your death line? (deadline)
- Next week I shall become a new car. (get)

Japan

- I have split up my boyfriend.
- I work hardly ten hours a day. (hard)

Portugal

- What will you do when you retire? I will breed with my horses.

Sweden

- Are you hopeful for any change? No, I am hopeless.

Finland

- How old is your son? Half past seven.

These mishaps happened on an almost daily basis when I worked in aviation. I recall crewing a flight where one passenger enthusiastically told me, 'My wife is a cow and I am a vegetable.' I duly acknowledged his meal request. Another passenger demanded water from one of my colleagues. She asked him light-heartedly, 'What's the magic word?' to which he replied, 'Abracadabra.' On another flight, a Korean crew member landed in Glasgow and was asked by a Scottish member of the ground staff, 'How was your shift?' She did not know how to respond, as she understood this term to refer to the motion of an object. While I explained this to her, another crew member volunteered that 'shift' means French kissing in Ireland. And then there are the written mishaps which can be around for perpetuity – I once received an email that ended 'hoping to hear from your esteemed end'. Just some of the valuable lessons of this early part of my career.

> The single biggest problem in communication is the illusion that it has taken place.
> – GEORGE BERNARD SHAW

Dividends from diversity

Given the intensely international nature of most larger businesses, companies are finding they need much greater diversity in their decision-making ranks. The diversity of the top leadership – its management and board of directors – should reflect the diversity of its employee base and customers. Transcending borders in leadership is not easy, but it is worth embracing. Here are some of the advantages of globally diverse teams:

- Versatility in problem-solving
- Fewer assumptions
- Different cognitive styles
- Better critical analysis
- Creativity
- Better response to cultural preferences in local markets
- Broader perspectives, less emphasis on conformity
- Better product design
- Bi- and multilinguals have a higher level of divergent thinking
- Better tolerance for ambiguity and chaos
- More charisma, stimulation and meaningful dialogue

No longer is it sufficient for leaders to meet the demands of shareholders and the laws and ethics of their home markets without regard for the negative consequences their business may have for the countries in which they operate. Today, conscious leaders guide their organisations to become partners with local governments to support the progress in their society, while operating within the legal framework. They take a holistic view of the organisation, and recognise that their stakeholders are not only their colleagues, but also their suppliers, partners, customers, shareholders and the environment at large in which the organisation operates.

Conscious leaders are required to grasp and bring clarity to a complex situation, while drawing people together, not pulling them apart. Alignment is built around the firm's purpose and values, which become the glue that binds the organisation together. This is in contrast to the traditional multinational and export structures, which are built around policies and rules-based management structures. Of course, organisations must have clear sets of rules and policies, but it is the purpose and values that are predominant. Ex-CEO of IBM Sam Palmisano stated:

> In a world of intense scrutiny, one reaction is to create more management systems, processes, controls, and more bureaucracy. Relying on traditional supervision, processes and controls would inhibit serving clients responsively, and stifle employees' creative energies. We cannot apply industrial-age management systems to address post-industrial-age needs. There is a better alternative, which is to trust employees. Values are the glue, the bond that binds us together in the absence of controls. These must be genuinely shared values; they can't be imposed top-down. Values provide employees a framework in which to make decisions when management systems and procedures are unclear. It comes down to judgement, based on shared values.

Today's corporate training programmes are not the solution. While they have evolved from indoctrinating rising executives in the company's *modus operandi* to addressing personal values and human qualities, the ability to incorporate these insights into daily working practices remains an issue.

There are many forms and styles of leadership. These five characteristics are shared by conscious leaders:

Self-awareness: Conscious leaders understand themselves at a deeper level – their strengths, vulnerabilities and biases. The key to their self-awareness lies in understanding the dominant paradigms in which they grew up. They are also aware of their own core values in life, and demonstrate a high level of humility and readiness to be guided by different cultural norms, as well as recognising that other cultures often have better ways of doing things.

Global curiosity: Conscious leaders have a deep curiosity about different cultures and a will to understand how they operate. This requires personal openness to a diversity of experience and a readiness to embrace humanity as a whole. Curiosity creates a drive to break down barriers, challenge traditional thinking and be willing to learn from failure. The curious leader fosters creativity and experimentation, and is always ready to ask 'Why?' and 'What if?'.

Empathy: Conscious leaders appreciate cultural norms and have the ability to walk (and then stand) in someone else's shoes. Empathy is about realising that we are all connected. This requires the ability to engage people from different cultures on their own terms, rather than standing back and judging them. Empathy inspires leaders to build rapport, to bond on a human level and to create lasting relationships. By being attuned to themselves and the world around them, conscious leaders are able to escape the confines of the rule book and parse out the deeper meaning in a given situation.

Collaboration: Partnerships are required in the future of leadership. Innovation in complex systems requires us to connect with the various stakeholders about the issues that matter to them. This means that single-focus approaches are almost certain to fail. Conscious leaders have mastered the art of broadening and deepening the definition of the problem (the problem beneath the problem) to get all of the relevant parties – who need one another if they are to change any system – committed to participating in the process.

Alignment: Conscious leaders see the bigger picture. They act as leader coaches and facilitators, probing deeper and actively seeking out divergent thinking before aligning around a decision or goal. After all, people need to *weigh* in before they *buy* in. They align employees around the company's purpose and values – a commitment that transcends national and cultural differences, although it is certainly *not* about achieving unanimity, and nor should it threaten to suppress individualism.

A new breed of leader

We should not confuse being in charge with being a leader. Being able to sustain success in this VUCA (volatile, uncertain, complex, ambiguous) world requires a change in our understanding of leadership from being about an individual to being about everyone, and dropping the unhelpful thinking that leadership is about having and communicating an opinion.

If we think we have been promoted on the strength of our opinions, then we automatically create a parent–child dynamic with our employees, as we believe they will look to our opinion on everything. In this unhealthy dynamic of giving and receiving opinions, we are missing out on the opportunity to tap into the potential of each person's humanity and co-create something meaningful for the future.

Just by listening, we build a sense of togetherness, and foster trust and respect. Think of those times when you shared a problem with someone and they chose not to come back with an immediate response. They saw you and took time to understand you. What happened? How was that for you?

How we show up as leaders – how we listen and connect, how we give and receive support, how we care for others – these are not just commitments. They are skills.

Gallup has been tracking employee engagement since the beginning of the century. During that time, less than one-third of employees in the world have been 'engaged' at work, and according to a recent Global State of the Workplace report, the figure could be as low as 13%. This should come as no surprise. As human beings, we have a fundamental need to be seen before we are heard and before we are spoken to.

During COVID-19, employees will have been forming beliefs about their company and their place within it which will inform how they show up afterwards:

- 'I am integral to this team' or 'I am dispensable'.
- 'I am valued' or 'I am just a number'.
- 'I am connected to a bigger purpose' or 'I am doing something meaningless'.

People only care how much you *know* when they *know* how much you care. It is about bringing humanity and accountability into the workplace. If this is achieved, employees will be able to bring their full and authentic selves to work, be more committed to their company and deliver better outcomes for customers.

The power of humanity at work

The front door of my home recently broke. It was a bit of a mystery, as we could not get in even after the professionals had broken the locking mechanism. Where I live, I have two neighbours – one who lives across from me, and the other to the side. It took fifteen people nine hours to break down the door. During that time, the neighbour opposite sat with us in the corridor to talk, offered the key to her apartment, made sure we were fed and watered. She was there when I needed it. She came to me.

The other neighbour saw the commotion and shouted down the corridor, 'Are you locked out?' I replied, 'Actually no, but we just can't get in.' He said, 'Please let me know if there is anything you need,' as the door closed behind him. Just like so many leaders I have encountered. 'Come and see me anytime – my door is always open,' they say. But they say these words without engaging their humanity.

Mahatma Gandhi's famous edict reminds us, 'For things to change, first I must change.' We need to raise our consciousness if we are really to see other people, and step out of our armour in order to be seen by them as fully human.

So how do we engage our humanity at work?

It does not have to involve grand gestures. Perhaps you will say 'good morning' to someone who usually goes unseen. It could even be holding the door for someone rushing or sharing a smile with a stranger. It is putting your phone away in meetings or as you walk between them or stand in the lift.

It is waiting to hear the answer to 'How are you today?', sending a message of thanks or sharing your perspective last in team meetings. It is suspending your expertise in order to build a non-judgemental relationship with others, listening with empathy so people know they have been heard and understood.

Perhaps it is adopting another's internal frame of reference and thereby opening up the possibility of 'real' conversation, by exchanging 'I disagree' for 'I have a different perspective'. It could be exploring eight of the most powerful words in leadership: 'I'm sorry, please, thank you, I don't know'.

> Curiosity is the 'open sesame' to
> learning, even for managers.
> – RUSSELL ACKOFF

It takes courage to step into a new territory, but these simple acts of kindness are contagious. Bring this consciousness into your conversations, lunches with colleagues and work projects to deepen your self-awareness. On your journey, let curiosity be your friend.

Like you, I imagine, I have had my fair share of terrible customer-service encounters. I recently went to the opening night of a new opera house. They would have benefitted from a soft launch, as it was a catalogue of disasters, all of which make me smile today. Having been raised in the heat of the Middle East, I can usually be found hanging out in shorts and flip-flops. That night, however, I dressed to the nines. I got out of the taxi and walked with my friend in her ballgown to the dimly lit entrance of the opera house, whereupon the fountain, which was built into the pavement, erupted through holes in the ground. We were drenched.

In the intermission, we grabbed a drink and foolishly rested it on the wobbly bar table. It wasn't long before the bottle of red wine toppled all over me. While laughing (a very British thing to do in these situations), I called over one of the staff. She said, 'Yes, can I help you?' She did not even seem to have registered that I was covered in red wine. I asked, 'Do you have any wet towels?' The reply was, 'No, we don't have any of those.' I settled for dry towels and used my bottled water to create the desired effect.

As we went to re-enter the concert hall, my friend (who was now dry from the fountain incident, but wet from the red wine one) said, 'Let me just wash my hands.' I waited near the usherette for those 60 seconds, exchanging the occasional silent glance. By the time my friend was back, the usherette said she had decided to close the doors and would not allow us to enter. Upon questioning the decision, we were told that she was just following the rules, having received special training designed to educate people in that part of the world about how opera works.

Before we left, the manager asked me what could be done to make everything all right. I simply encouraged her to bring her humanity more overtly into her work, so that her team could bring theirs. As I went to the taxi rank (avoiding the fountain) for my carriage home, I was reminded of Cinderella's motto: 'Have courage and be kind.' All the trainings and briefings in the world could probably help little to resolve the mess until and unless the leader introduced more common humanity into the process.

In that sense, the question for leaders is not 'What can we *do* now?', it is 'Who do we need to *be*?' in order to create the shift.

When we *express* our humanity, we are far more likely to *feel* our humanity. If we truly see and hear people, it is more likely that they will live their values and do the right thing. And it is no doubt good for the bottom line, as people show up more fully and hence make a more valuable contribution. Conscious leaders give their whole being – and receive the same in return.

And this becomes your legacy. Herb Kelleher always said 'the business of business is people'. His airline, Southwest, enjoyed 47 years of consecutive profit in an environment of deregulation, fuel shocks, air-traffic controller strikes, crippling recessions, interest-rate spikes and hijackings.

Remembering Herb, Southwest Airline's CEO, Gary Kelly, talked about what great leaders leave behind. 'It's been said that legacy is not leaving something for people – like things – it's leaving something *in* people. *That* is what Herb did.'

He is right. Conscious leaders show us what is possible and illuminate the great heights to which we can rise. And we can effect whole-system change when we become aware of the subtle web of relationships and the hidden forces and patterns in play, as well as our own place within the system.

Illuminating Systems

Out beyond ideas of wrongdoing and right
doing there is a field. I'll meet you there.
— RUMI

So how to become more conscious of the big picture, seeing and understanding it in a way that clarifies how we and all its various parts fit together? If we deal with an issue through a merely linear approach, the solution may appear to work at first, but soon the inertia or difficulty will return, often deepening and expanding, until a systems perspective and methodology are used to resolve it.

Issues that lie within the multiple dynamics of a complex system do not get resolved by increased emotional or global intelligence alone. These are not enough to resolve the dynamics of complex interpersonal relations, cognitive blind spots, unconscious behavioural patterns and habitual mental responses. Such issues are too much for one style of leadership or one leadership model to handle.

> Invisible threads are the strongest ties.
> – FRIEDRICH NIETZSCHE

In *Systemic Coaching and Constellations*, John Whittington explains how a system perspective can provide an alternative way of looking at things that can liberate energy and offer fresh clarity across complex systems.

Systemic coaching is a practical and respectful approach that can create lasting, positive change, and can be applied to individuals, teams, groups, organisations and communities. It brings a framework for exploring, clarifying and resolving different types of leadership, team and organisational issues.

By using 'constellations' one can look at the hidden structure that underlies a relationship system. This then illuminates invisible loyalties and reveals unseen psychological and energetic ties, as well as the sources of challenging behaviour and resistance to change. Such an approach allows people to go beyond words and out of the purely intellectual space, accessing the embodied tacit information that exists in all systems and using various scenarios to test how such resources might best be deployed.

Secrets and solutions

    I worked with a chief executive who was
    facing into the most challenging crisis
    of his leadership. We decided to get out

of the city and go for a walk in the forest, using nature to represent his system in the three-dimensional world. That is the beauty of this work: it moves hidden dynamics into plain sight. At the end of our journey, we grew tired and were confronted by a tree in the middle of our path that had died (in systemics everything is viewed as information). The roots, however, must have had enough fuel from food left in them to produce sprouts from the remains of the trunk. It looked as if the sprouts on the stump wanted to develop more leaves and grow into a new tree; they just needed the right conditions.

That night my client visited his mother to share some of the insights from our walk. She revealed a secret that had lain hidden in their family system for 30 years. Unbeknownst to him, his late father was made redundant by the predecessor of the company that he now led, which had caused shame and significant hardship throughout his upbringing. His father would pretend to go to work, but actually spend his days in various places – including the pub – in his suit and tie until it was time to go home.

Challenging exits that do not respectfully honour the bonds that are broken through lost membership, and fail to acknowledge what was gained and what was lost, create ties and entanglements that can reach forward for many years, through many systems, leaving a messy knot of unresolved dynamics. In my experience, all organisational systems have their roots in family systems. Once my client's unwitting entanglement in his past was revealed, he was able to move forward. He left behind what had belonged to his father, and took with him what was his own. He wrote a letter to his late father asking him to smile on him as he made a success of his leadership role. To this day, he and his company are thriving.

How difficulties manifest often depends on whether or not we recognise what the situation needs to reveal to us about ourselves. Even if the person who suffered the original trauma has died, or the story has been forgotten or silenced, memory and feelings can live on. These emotional legacies are believed to play a far greater role in our emotional and physical health than has ever before been understood. A recent and provocative claim is that the experience of trauma – or more accurately the effect of that experience – is 'passed' somehow from one generation to the next through non-genomic, possibly epigenetic mechanisms, affecting DNA function or gene transcription. Rachel Yehuda, PhD, professor of psychiatry and neuroscience and director of traumatic stress studies at the Icahn School of Medicine at Mount Sinai, is pioneering research into understanding the mechanisms that underlie the phenomenon of intergenerational and transgenerational transmission.

The principles of systems

The principles of time, place and exchange are products of the systemic conscience, which tries to maintain coherence and balance at all times. If one or more of these three principles is ignored, this will often prove to be the root cause of inertia or stuckness in the system, and will manifest as dysfunction or conflict.

> The world is not to be put in order,
> the world is order. It is for us to put
> ourselves in unison with this order.
> – HENRY MILLER

Time

- Those who joined the system first need to be acknowledged before those who follow can find their place and fully occupy their role.
- When a new leader joins with a recognition that they are the last in place in the context of *time*, they are able to advance freely in the system.
- Acknowledgement of who contributed first (e.g. the founders or previous role holder) generates clarity, order and flow in the system.
- Application of this principle releases energy in systems and allows the past to stay where it belongs – in the past. The system can then move into the future.

```
As  the  younger  of  two  siblings,  it  was
not  until  I  recognised  my  sister's  role
as  the  elder  child  that  we  were  able  to
```

enjoy a strong relationship, which brought
a revitalised energy to my leadership. The
principle of time also applies to pregnancy
loss or abortion, where an unborn baby must
be acknowledged in order for those who are
living to be able to flow fully.

Place

- Everybody in a system has an equal right to belong. When that right is denied by exclusion, the system will attempt to 're-member' them until their *place* and contribution are acknowledged.
- People who leave systems under difficult circumstances leave unresolved problems in place such that they recreate those patterns in the next system they enter.
- Exclusion draws the energy and focus out of the system.
- Organisations spend significant amounts of time and money excluding people who formerly belonged to a system.

It was only through a constellation that
I was able to see that I was recreat-
ing patterns of exclusion in every system to which I belonged, and that I was
doing this because I was separated from
my father at the age of eight. Whether
through a teacher or a boss, the system
was trying to illuminate the cause of the

dysfunction until I acknowledged it and honoured my parents for the choices they had made. At that point, I was able to hold my place in those systems.

Exchange

- There needs to be a continuous balancing of giving and receiving between all parts of a system for it to remain in flow.
- An imbalance of *exchange* is often present in corporate life between parts of the system. The impact of this dynamic is also felt by talent, where their over-giving creates an imbalance in the system they are interacting with, which can weaken the client and the whole system.
- A violation of this organising principle is also seen in mergers and acquisitions, and often lies at the root of later difficulties.
- An imbalance creates deeper and less healthy bonding than balance.

I subconsciously tried to adopt the role of father figure when my mum moved to the UK with my sister and me. I took this unhealthy dynamic into my leadership, overcompensating at every opportunity to be the saviour, and denying myself help and support. Through my own systemic constellation, I was able to recognise the enmeshment, leaving with my father what was his and taking

```
with me what is mine, freeing us both from
the entanglement and allowing exchange to
be free-flowing again.
```

Judge not, but acknowledge – and you shall see

The principle of acknowledgement runs through systemic coaching and the application of constellations. When we acknowledge what is just as it is, without any judgement, what emerges is an understanding of the interconnected nature of everything and everyone in systems.

In a healthy system, there is no shame about difficult events in the past, and nobody who has made a contribution to the system is forgotten or excluded.

Humanity needs to break the shackles of the current system

If we consciously decide that we do not want to belong in a particular system – that we do not want to be like 'them' – we are likely to end up becoming...just like them. In systemics, whatever we exclude, we attract. And what we judge, we become.

For us to grow, we first have to acknowledge our belonging and what we gained from it. If we do not feel ready or able to acknowledge what we received from the system to which we belonged, we may find ourselves looking back with resentment.

When we more fully understand the different systems that surround us, we can uncover new opportunities and, where needed, find resolution. We move from building more skills and knowledge to increasing consciousness and resourcefulness – from problem-solving to the deeper skills of identifying patterns and resolving dilemmas. Deeper truths and loyalties emerge for humanity, releasing individuals, groups and teams to flow freely again.

Leading from the perspective of systemic awareness does not require us to agree *with* everything. We simply need to agree *to* everything as it is. The judgements of 'good' and 'bad' – of 'right' and 'wrong' – do not apply when perceiving systems, if we wish to understand them and how they function – or malfunction. There is only 'what is'. Such a systemic awareness enables us respectfully to recognise there is a reason for everything that is presenting itself to us (and wanting to reveal/reflect back something about ourselves). Looking at it all with compassion for belonging and an understanding of loyalty changes our perspective. It has profound implications for business and society, as I found out as a 16-year-old boy in China.

Lessons from the East

When I let go of what I am, I
become what I might be.
– Lao Tzu

spent most of secondary school being bullied. It was an all-boys school that ticked every box if you excelled in rugby and your parents had high ambitions of you going to Oxbridge. Some of my teachers were even involved in the bullying. In a year of 213 boys, 211 were made prefects, one appointed head boy and I was excluded.

It sounds trite to say that I am grateful to the bullies, but they certainly taught me resilience and gave me the opportunity to practise forgiveness. I do wonder if I would have more hair today if I had not spent so much time with my head being flushed down toilets!

I just wish someone could have told me when I was younger that it is OK not to conform. Because I never felt as though I fitted in, I grew comfortable sitting on the periphery of systems. I had nothing to lose, so I embraced being a non-conformist. I am pretty sure you are reading this book because you are a non-conformist too – the people who create purposeful change in businesses and communities usually are.

My school was nestled under the flight path of Manchester Airport. At 16, I remember looking out of the arched window on a frosty February afternoon, desperate to escape my dire situation. The school resembled Hogwarts, but instead of a broom flying by, there was a Cathay Pacific 747 soaring past.

By that time, I had been studying Eastern philosophies and religions for five years and I already had a deep inner knowing that I needed to go to Asia. It was the Friday before the half-term holidays. When I got home, I sat my mum down and asked (begged) her to let me travel the next day to Asia. Amazingly, she acquiesced.

Having lived in different countries all my life, I really did not think anything of it, until I was standing in the immigration queue on arrival in China and wondering what to tell the officer if he asked me with whom I was staying. Thankfully, I was allowed in, and my adventure took me all across the country – a very different place in the mid-'90s. It was from this trip that I realised how much we could learn by opening our hearts and minds to different philosophies and traditions.

The way of the Dao

Daoism, also known as Taoism, is an ancient Chinese philosophy based on the writings of Lao-Tzu which advocates simple living and harmony with nature. Dao is the process of reality itself, the way things hold together while still transforming themselves, the perpetual process of subtle change and course correction required to maintain overall harmony. All this reflects the deep-seated belief that changeableness is the most basic character of things.

Some of the best-known principles of Daoism include:

First principle: Sometimes translated as 'Oneness', the first principle states that everything in nature is part of the same whole. We are intricately linked to it and created by it through a sort of existential force. The central teaching of Daoism is that human beings can fulfil their highest goal by achieving integration with nature, thereby becoming one with the Dao and contributing to cosmic harmony.

Yin-yang: In Daoism, the yin-yang classification suggests the idea that differences are needed in order for harmony to exist. Correlatives in Chinese philosophy are not opposites, mutually excluding each other. They represent the ebb and flow of the forces of reality: yin/yang, male/female; excess/lack; leading/following; active/passive. As one approaches the fullness of yin, yang begins to emerge on the horizon, and vice versa.

Wu wei: Wu wei is often considered the most important of all the Daoist beliefs. Often translated as 'non-action', wu wei is the idea that one should not overreact or over-plan in any situation. It is the idea that actions should come naturally, that we should be spontaneous, taking life as it comes to us, doing what is necessary in the moment. Water exemplifies the philosophy of wu wei. Water does not resist, but by the same token, it can be a powerful and mighty force that carries away life in its current; in other words, action without reaction.

In his book *The Tao of the West*, JJ Clarke writes that the Dao can be construed as a feminine reality, a maternal, life-producing energy. Daoism, along with other Asian systems, represents an enlightened alternative to Western patriarchal attitudes, or to its antagonistic dualisms. It is a philosophy that helps conceptualise the human self and relationships in ways which honour holistic integration, interrelatedness, caring and love. It is not intended to substitute the feminine for the masculine, but to restore the equilibrium, which is the natural way of the Dao.

Daoism represents an image of human connectedness and non-aggressive harmony that contrasts with the masculine values of assertive independence and competitiveness that have typified modern Western cultural attitudes. Daoist understanding is not based on a high estimation of the virtues of meekness and humility – it does not place these qualities higher than their opposites – but rather on the belief that aggression is a form of weakness, not of strength, and that the yin power of passivity is more enduring than, and therefore ultimately just as effective as, the yang force of direct action.

Daoism is emerging as a reticent yet increasingly visible player in contemporary culture, and has become a site of cultural transformation and spiritual creativity that is beginning to operate globally at many levels. Some of its manifestations can already be observed alongside other intellectual and religious products – the vogue for feng shui and the popularity of the taiji symbol providing obvious examples of this phenomenon.

We can learn from Daoism to back away from confrontation and to prefer accommodation and mutual harmony over self-assertiveness and aggressive contentiousness. The objective of this way of thinking is to bring about a change of attitude that will free humanity from the confines of our narrow perspective, and engender a kind of open-mindedness that consists of becoming less opinionated, recognising that all opinions, perspectives and beliefs are, by their nature, always partially right and partially wrong. It is just a matter of degree.

The task that humanity faces is to create a framework of ideas and values that will facilitate the harmonious co-existence of different beliefs and encourage the flourishing of divergent ways of thinking and being. The spirit of the Zhuangzi is, 'You can't discuss the Way with a cramped scholar – he's shackled by his doctrines.'

Working with the Dao

Daoism has the potential to show us what the new paradigm of conscious leadership looks like:

Wholeness

Instead of showing only their narrow 'professional' selves, organisations of the future will invite people to reclaim their inner wholeness. They will create an environment wherein people feel free to fully express themselves, bringing unprecedented levels of authentic energy, passion and creativity to work.

Self-management

In the future of work, organisations will operate effectively, even at a large scale, with a system based on peer relationships. They will set up structures and practices in which people enjoy significant levels of autonomy, while also being accountable. Power and control will no longer be tied to the specific positions of a few top leaders. The truth is, we are all leaders.

> 'A leader is best when people barely know he exists, when his work is done, they will say: we did it ourselves.'
> – Lao Tzu

Evolutionary purpose

Organisations will operate more like organisms, basing their strategies on what they sense the world is asking from them. Agile practices that sense and respond replace the machinery of line-manager approvals, targets and incentives. Paradoxically, by focusing less on the bottom line and shareholder value, they generate better financial results for the long term.

In the new paradigm, founders and leaders view the organism as a living entity with its own energy, sense of direction and calling to manifest something in the world. They do not force a course of action; they try to listen to where the organisation is naturally called to go. Gone will be the dreaded strategy formulation exercises, midterm plans, yearly budgets, cascaded KPIs and individual targets. Instead of trying to predict and control, conscious leaders will aim to sense and respond, moving from teachers to 'sensei', the latter judged by their humanity above their martial arts skills.

In this system, change can come from any person who senses that change is needed. This is how change has occurred in nature for millions of years. Innovation does not happen centrally, from the top, according to plan, but at the edges, when an organism senses a change in the environment and experiments to find an appropriate response. Some attempts fail to catch on; others rapidly spread to all corners of the ecosystem. They are more resilient as a result. It is nearer to what Martin Heidegger calls 'releasement', a letting go of things, rather than always seeking to transform them and to impose intellectual conformity on nature, or lapsing into despair if this proves impossible.

The study of other cultures, languages, traditions and philosophies can provide us with the potential for unlearning our own conceptual habits, to recover important things lost in the progress of civilisation. A 'being towards stillness' that embraces and celebrates wholeness: this may be the wisest lesson that I took from the first of my many adventures in the East.

Becoming Whole

We are not meant to be perfect,
we are meant to be whole.
– JANE FONDA

Regardless of our gender, each one of us contains both 'masculine' and 'feminine' energy. While it is the 'essence' of the male sex – an individual in a biologically male bodysuit – to have traditional masculine traits dominant (because of the conditions created by that flavour of bodysuit), and vice versa, this will never be to the exclusion of the balancing traits associated with the opposite gender. In order to function as a full human being it is essential to have all traits present – and to use them all, as and where appropriate, regardless of an individual's outer appearance or identity. All ancient and esoteric traditions have recognised this, while characterising the feminine energy as the yin, lunar, Shakti or receptive principle, while masculine energy is the yang, solar, Shiva or active principle. But both are always understood to be present in individuals of all genders.

Our out-of-balance working world

For the longest time, we have been told to show up as analytical, competitive and driven in order to appear 'successful' at work. Numbers, money and status were all-important, and the way to achieve them was through ambition and rapid growth. When we examine the underlying cultural norms or expectations that are driving observable behaviour, we find that one of the most engrained and unconsciously accepted is the emphasis placed on the goal, which is a masculine trait. Feminine cultures place more emphasis on the process towards that goal. The problem with this masculine norm is that when we are too focused on the goal, it creates blind spots and comes at the cost of our other responsibilities.

Change, as we experience it in corporations, is masculine (focus, drive, action), but bringing it to life also requires feminine attributes (empathy, vulnerability-based trust, relationship-building and open communication). While deep listening, collaboration, flexibility and empathy feature in most leadership training programmes, cultural norms back at the office usually dictate that these qualities are not truly valued and therefore do not stick.

And because of unconscious bias, the same leadership traits can be perceived differently in men and in women. Notice how the word 'boss' is masculine and celebrated in men – the same trait in women is deemed 'bossy'. 'Emotional' in women is 'passionate' for men, 'feisty' women make 'determined' men, 'abrasion' is seen as 'assertion', and 'calculating' becomes 'strategic'.

It is understandable, therefore, why we might mask and suppress parts of ourselves, in order to fit in and conform to accepted norms at work. Over time, though, if we don't bring the totality of our selves, our essence dissolves. What a delicate tightrope we created in leadership – worrying about how to be enough of something, but never too much.

Hegemonic masculinity

As we have seen, patriarchal forces and capitalist power structures in the West have stopped honouring the feminine, creating the perception that the masculine route of conquest and takeovers is the only way to succeed. Though men benefit from this patriarchy, they are impinged upon by it too.

In 2018, the American Psychological Association (APA) published the *APA Guidelines for Psychological Practice with Boys and Men*. Thirteen years in the making, it draws on more than forty years of research showing that traditional masculinity is psychologically harmful, and that socialising boys to suppress their emotions causes damage to mental and physical health.

Fredric Rabinowitz, PhD, a psychologist at the University of Redlands in California who has stewarded the new guidelines, stated:

Because of the way many men have been brought up – to be self-sufficient and able to take care of themselves – any sense that things aren't OK needs to be kept secret. Part of what happens is men who keep things to themselves look outward and see that no one else is sharing any of the conflicts that they feel inside. That makes them feel isolated. They think they're alone. They think they're weak. They think they're not OK. They don't realise that other men are also harbouring private thoughts and private emotions and private conflicts.

Hegemonic masculinity marginalises men who do not perfectly fit the description of a 'real man'. Because no man perfectly fits that description, all men are limited, through policing of behaviours seen as 'violations'.

Think about your own life. Have you ever been told to 'toughen up' or 'not be so emotional at work'? This vague 'feedback' is often a euphemism for not being masculine enough, with the subtext that we should assert ourselves, be louder or be less sensitive. I have been abused by men I don't even know for wearing pink swimming shorts and owning a cat instead of a dog; and I have seen men ridiculed for crying or openly declaring their love for a partner. I was in the presence of someone who was told to 'toughen up, princess' when vulnerably sharing their feelings of being low, before being handed another beer.

The unintended side effects are enormous. Suicide is the single biggest killer of men under the age of 45 in the UK. Compared to women, men are three times more likely to die by suicide in Australia, 3.5 times more likely in the US and more than four times more likely in Russia and Argentina.

Restoring the balance

Clinical psychologist Professor Jordan Peterson argues that feminine traits in business do not predict success in the market. In fact, he suggests that 'agreeableness' negatively predicts success in the workplace. The empirical evidence shows that masculine traits are helpful to succeed in the current paradigm. Professor Peterson admits that if companies modified their behaviour and became more feminine, they could be successful, but there is currently no evidence for it. Perhaps it is time to run this experiment and be non-agreeable to being non-agreeable!

Let us emphasise that this is not about gender. All of us are at our best when our energies are in balance, when we are able to use either set of energies in accord with what is appropriate. People who lead with balanced energy tap into a unique source of power – those with whom they interact find it very disarming (in a positive way!).

Such wholeness lends itself to compassionate, rational ways of thinking that enhance relationships with others by appreciating and valuing their different perspectives. It enables us to have strong opinions while holding them lightly, staying vigilant yet vulnerable, with strength and gentleness, courage and kindness. It promotes inclusion and creativity just as much as delivery and execution. The ability to hold these opposing vibrations and find harmony is already within us. The world turns differently when fire loves water. Everything flows.

In healthy systems people want to make a full contribution because they know they are doing something that will be valued and have an impact as part of a whole – a whole that can achieve things that are more than the sum of its parts. But when health is absent, so are the people. Individuals who are unsure of their place or their role in the system cannot be fully present and so do not bring their full self into their work. They withhold something, unconsciously resisting a fuller contribution. Trust and motivation are missing or unreliable.

The answer to today's problems is not to eschew masculinity and over-value the feminine. The answer is for us to get to a stage where we just see these as 'human' qualities – and all of them as equally valuable at different times.

> If we divide human attributes into 'masculine' and 'feminine' and strengthen only those attributes that 'belong' to that sex, we cut off half of ourselves from ourselves as human beings, condemned forever to search for our other half. The world is in desperate need of multi-layered human beings with the voices,

stamina and insight to break through our
current calcified ways of doing things.
– Tina Packer

Perhaps the greatest risk any of us will ever take is to be seen as we really are. Nevertheless, I invite you to take that risk and express your humanity to the world.

Shift your energy, and the energy of the whole world will shift too. As we will see in the next chapter, it has never been more important to do so.

When 'Progress' Isn't

Science is a beautiful gift to humanity;
we should not distort it.
– APJ ABDUL KALAM

t is predicted that the next 20 years will see more change than the last 200. According to journalist Graeme Wood, change has never happened this fast before and will never be this slow again. The impact this will have on societal norms cannot be underestimated. AI-driven machines are about to make one of humanity's oldest activities much weirder – the sex robots are here!

The lost side of the argument

Intelligent debates about technology are often shut down. And in communities where people are supposed to be able to discuss things, the barrage of propaganda from Silicon Valley makes anyone who chooses not to peddle the narrative a 'hater' or 'denier'. The powerful always defend the status quo because it is the source of their privilege. Kübler-Ross's model of the five stages of grief is even misapplied to 'luddites' who question the narrative, so that they are presented as being in the denial, anger, depression or bargaining stage, before finally reaching acceptance. This, we are told, is our reality and we must accept it. Peter Hinssen, author of *The Day After Tomorrow*, says that Europe will never have a Silicon Valley because of 'European questions' that always start with, 'Yes, but…' Thank goodness.

Artificial intelligence has the potential to enhance human beings' capability beyond our imagination. But technology has eroded our ability to have meaningful debates about the very same subject, which is unsurprising given that we have been able to hide behind the black mirror of our screens for so much of this century.

Futurists assure us that mass unemployment is overstated, and that AI will free up humanity to focus on culture, arts, creativity, philosophy, exploration and adventure. But as more jobs are automated, where will we be getting taxable income from? Some say we will tax the robots, yet governments currently struggle to impose even arbitrary taxes on big tech firms.

Without meaningful values, are you confident that business leaders, driven by share price and quarterly reporting – the unnatural consequence of IPOs – are going to put humanity above the efficiency gains and cost savings that automation brings? When the CEO of ING announced plans to shed 7,000 jobs to accelerate the bank's 'Think Forward' strategy, Ike Wiersinga of the Dutch CNV union commented, 'I don't think this was the intention of the [government] when it kept ING afloat with bailout money.'

Lost in the seduction of digitalisation, we fail to see what else is going on. We overwork people until they burn out, accuse them of being inferior and then justify replacing them with machines that do not get tired. To take away the possibility of meaningful employment will bring unknown societal issues. It is innate in humanity to contribute, to do something useful and make other people's lives better. Decades after mines in Britain were shut down, the 'unhappy valleys' of South Wales still have the highest prescription rates for antidepressant pills in the UK.

Who polices the police?

With every e-mail we send, every Skype call, every tweet, every book we buy, our data is being extracted and fed into the big technology companies. How has humanity got to the point where we are beholden to technology, intertwined with profit maximisation?

A tweet from *Mastercardnews* speaks to the tone-deafness when it comes to privacy:

Voting, driving, applying for a job, renting a home, getting married and boarding a plane: what do these all have in common? You need to prove your identity. In partnership with @Microsoft, we are working to create universally recognised digital identity.

Euphemism for universal tracking of users. To the corporations, this is a brilliant solution. To the rest of us, it may feel more than a bit dystopian, as we creep to inhumane levels of top-down control, and edge from soft authoritarianism towards totalitarianism. Meanwhile, distracted by the very same technology, we willingly allow the devices into our homes and bedrooms to survey and gather data on us.

In 2018, Cambridge Analytica was accused of illicitly harvesting the data of 87 million people from Facebook to profile people politically so that it could better target them with Facebook ads ahead of the Brexit referendum. The UK parliament asked Mark Zuckerberg to come to Britain and account for the activities of his network, but he refused multiple times. As reporter Carole Cadwalladr told the 'gods of Silicon Valley', 'You set out to connect people. And you are refusing to acknowledge that the same technology is now driving us apart.'

Few realise just how much personal data is being captured. A friend of mine came over to my place on my birthday. She joked (I hope!) that she had contemplated getting me a Botox appointment for a present. My phone must have been lying around the house somewhere. Surprise, surprise, the next day advertisements of local Botox clinics appeared on my social media feed. I immediately switched off the voice-controlled functions on my devices, but I would be foolish to believe this is about me regaining my individual rights. We are beyond a story about an individual social contract with companies. Most of the trillions of data points have nothing to do with what we knowingly give – these are metadata that are lifted from aspects of our experience in ways that are designed to bypass our awareness.

The same companies are now censoring the information that we are allowed to receive. To tackle 'misinformation', strict new company policies have been implemented. YouTube blocks 'anything that would go against World Health Organisation (WHO) recommendations'. Facebook now flags warnings on select posts – 'Your post goes against our Community Standards on misinformation that could cause physical harm' – and WhatsApp has introduced restrictions on 'frequently forwarded' messages with the intention of disrupting 'false claims'.

Science is an error-correcting process. It is the nature of scientific enquiry that scientists publish hypotheses for scrutiny and purposeful enquiry that may later be disproved by new evidence and replaced by a better rival. Current levels of censorship deny a platform to dissenting voices, and imply that humanity is incapable of thinking, checking different sources and making its own connections.

> Science becomes a source of authority
> rather than a mode of inquiry. The real
> utility of science stems from the latter; the
> political utility stems from the former.
> – PROFESSOR RICHARD LINDZEN

Most if not all dangerous movements in history started with the same pretext: 'for your own good'. What is emerging from the scientific community is that over the past 40 years scientists have not got funded or published if they did not toe the line. If we are to break the cycle, then we must keep our enquiring minds. Truth is learned, not told.

Is artificial efficiency really the answer – are we asking the right question?

Artificial intelligence can take care of the tedious tasks that human beings perform in order to achieve varied results. Let us take the example of the digital transformation of the banking sector. Online banking is infinitely quicker and easier for consumers. This could go a long way in helping financial analysts to focus on deeper research and an all-around improved customer experience.

But several companies are even replacing customer service positions with AI after top executives deemed people to be too inconsistent.

And yet, along with inconsistency come spontaneity, creative insight and, above all, the ability to handle situations that do not fit the boxes and forms to which automated consistency demands we all conform. And it is our spontaneity that makes us wonderful.

Humanity is able to improvise and respond to a specific situation appropriately when automation has failed. As a company owner, when I applied for a visa to visit India, the system required me to write a letter (no objection certificate) allowing me to travel. 'I, Samie, hereby allow Samie to travel. He/I will cover all costs...' Clearly, this is ridiculous, so I escalated to a person, who bypassed the requirement in an instant. Interestingly, the person assisting me said, 'It's the first time we've heard about this,' which made me wonder just how accustomed we have become to being dealt with by automated processes. Dimming our humanity again.

A rather tall gentleman recounted to me how he had reserved a bulkhead seat on a red-eye flight. Between the time of online booking and the date of travel, the company introduced an ancillary charge for those seats, so automatically relocated him to a middle seat at the back of the plane. This was only revealed at the time of online check-in, and there was no way of rectifying it on the system, as the seats were blocked. Thankfully, a conscious leader in the form of a call-centre agent showed empathy, understood that this was a situation where the rules should not apply and, guided by the company's values, reassigned the gentleman's seat without charge.

It may be easier for companies to go down the path of replacing customer service roles with AI than to embed meaningful values and evolve the organisational culture to inspire more moments of brilliance. The question is, where does that path lead us?

I recently sold my house and put the equity in the bank. One day I went into the banking app to make a transfer and noticed the entire amount had disappeared. I scrambled to find the telephone banking passcode that I so rarely use. Eight hours of calls later, I was told that I would be given an update within five working days. It was not possible for a supervisor to bypass the system – I had to wait for the computer to send notifications up chains of command known as 'levels'. A week later the funds arrived back in my account, along with £60 compensation for my time. AI might be more efficient, but is it more effective?

Barclays Bank ended up scrapping a 'limited pilot' of monitoring software to measure the productivity of its employees. The 'Big Brother-style' system tracked how long employees were at their desks, and sent warnings if they spent too long on breaks. A whistleblower reportedly said, 'The stress this is causing is beyond belief.'

This echoes the allegations from Amazon warehouses. The robots have helped the company fulfil its ever-increasing promises of speedy deliveries to customers, while monitoring and supervising human beings. Amazon's system tracks the rates of each individual associate's productivity and automatically generates any warnings regarding quality of productivity. Amazon says supervisors are able to override the process, and has since filmed TV commercials dedicated to how much employees love working at their 'fulfilment centres'.

The company might benefit from assigning more people to make sense of its core values, which include:

Frugality: accomplish more with less. Constraints breed resourcefulness, self-sufficiency, and invention. There are no extra points for growing headcount, budget size, or fixed expense.

Such humane intervention might have avoided the situation in which some Amazon employees were allegedly urinating in bottles at their work stations to maintain productivity targets.

The inhumanity of numbers

How pervasive is this problem of the invisible layer of decision-making and surveillance machines that are all around us, but not riding motorcycles like Arnold Schwarzenegger in *Terminator*? The burgeoning field of data analytics cannot help but get seduced by all its amazing numbers.

Without the human element, AI treats as certain something that remains ambiguous. We may think machines are learning, but assigning meaning to big data is a purely human function. Meaning-making is what defines us as human beings. AI points out for us probabilities, not certainties. The system can tell us yes/no/right/wrong, but what was the context? What was going on for the people being surveyed? For a person studying a given situation, meaning may emerge over time, as it evolves, at which point the entire process can be seen to make sense. AI would be incapable of interpreting in this way.

Let us take sentencing as an example. Precisely because it is objective, AI might rule in the same way for people who have committed several crimes and therefore have a likelihood of reoffending. But what if someone has stolen to feed their children? The system needs a human judge who has a capacity for compassion to apply appropriate meaning to the facts.

Can AI really know who we are and why we do what we do?

Profiling is a part of everyday life. Airport security, Facebook, Google, Amazon, insurance companies and supermarkets, among many others, use algorithms to categorise us and weigh up our potential for profit or risk. Of course there are good reasons for this, and advantages to the approach.

But if it leads to more widespread and invasive adaptation, as new technology often does, then adding facial recognition capabilities to CCTV cameras would be a game-changer. Given that the system inevitably processes the biometric data of everyone, live facial recognition – now standard on our phones – has the potential to fundamentally change the power relationship between people and the police – and even alter the very meaning of public space. Suddenly, the police could trace an individual as they moved across the city within seconds. And when the public are fearful, as is the case with coronavirus, we will be more likely to accept 'surveillance creep'. Progress which isn't.

Governments and scientists were united in their conviction that they needed much greater levels of 'tracking' for containing the coronavirus. US President Donald Trump was sure to mention the 'COVID-19 Screening Tool' app developed by Apple in a briefing during the outbreak. The question we should be asking: 'Where does the information people put into the app go and where is the accountability if something goes wrong?'

We should be concerned. On a recent call to an Apple Support manager regarding a bug that rendered my iPhone unusable, the manager recited to me the process that left me with no one above him to whom I might escalate the complaint. Left without recourse, I asked what my customer rights were. The manager concluded, 'If you don't like it, tell your government.' Maybe we will.

For the first time in history it has become feasible to monitor everybody all the time. It is no surprise to me that Amazon started out with books (remember those days?). Their data builds a psychological profile on us. If I know the ideas you are exposed to, where your influences come from, what you lean into, then I can control you. The system is learning about you and building a comprehensive profile of how you think, who you are and what you believe in when you are alone.

Once we go 'under the skin' and collect biometric data – the last bounty of personal data – the analysis will mean we are known by the system better than we know ourselves, as emotions and feelings are biological phenomena, just as a fever is. Big tech may be willing and able to take on the role of Big Brother, but those on the receiving end of a heavy-handed surveillance state are unlikely to care whether it is the public or private sector doing the oppressing.

Another pitfall of profiling is that it alienates marginalised groups and can easily lead to a breakdown of trust between these and other groups. Race equality campaigners have been spied upon, climate activists have been put on an extremism watch-list; even an elderly party conference heckler found himself held under terror laws. As the son of a Syrian, I recall the endless hours being questioned at airports in the United States, usually resulting in missed connections not covered by insurance. Ironically, it was a ninth-century Muslim scholar who gave English the term 'algorithm'!

Notably, in September 2018, Sir Tim Berners-Lee, inventor of the World Wide Web, stated that his early hopes for the World Wide Web have been dashed. He wrote:

I've always believed the web is for everyone. That's why I and others fight fiercely to protect it. The changes we've managed to bring have created a better and more connected world. But for all the good we've achieved, the web has evolved into an engine of inequity and division; swayed by powerful forces that use it for their own agendas...

Back to the bank that temporarily lost my life savings. Five days later, when I finally reached a person in customer service, I was advised that a mental-health marker could be placed on my account in response to the stress I had experienced. I did not need the help, but I also declined on the grounds that I did not know how the computers might then prejudge me in the future.

There is a positive role for predictive analytics, but we need to be aware of collective (pre)judgement or a sense of determinism. If the data is flawed by systematic historical cultural biases, those same biases will be replicated at scale. This is what happens when a major global industry such as computer programming is dominated by a singular cultural perspective. According to a Stack Overflow survey, 85.5% of computer programmers in the US are male, and the vast majority of those males are white. You cannot even avoid the bias by taking race out as a criterion, as if it is clever enough, the system will work it out by proxy – through home address, for example.

Amazon tried building an artificial-intelligence tool to help with recruiting, but it showed a bias against women. Engineers reportedly found the AI was unfavourable towards female candidates because it had combed through male-dominated résumés to accrue its data. The computer models were trained to vet applicants by observing patterns in résumés submitted to the company over a ten-year period. The technology also favoured candidates who described themselves using verbs more commonly found on male engineers' résumés such as 'executed' and 'captured'. Today, robots are getting away with what would be illegal if a human being operated that way.

In response, Microsoft has been exploring the ethical use of AI and has come up with six principles to ensure that actions taken are in our best interests. Though this is comforting at first glance, we must be careful about the role homogeny will play in defining our sensibilities, perspectives and priorities. Just think about it – programming that helps you do something best. 'Best' according to whom? I do not know about you, but I do not feel particularly represented by senior executives in business, or government ministers, or Facebook's 'independent' Oversight Board for that matter.

> 'The greatest treason of all is to do the
> right thing for the wrong reason.'
> – TS Eliot

As we saw in the chapter on conscious leadership, enlightened companies know that the strongest antidote to cultural bias is diversity – a diversity of minds, experiences, backgrounds, beliefs, languages and perspectives. This combined richness of intellect and creativity builds a synergy of influence that restricts the ability of cultural bias to determine the end result of the programming. Simply put, diversity is an inoculation.

Is every new technology a good idea?

Telecommunications companies worldwide, with the support of governments, have been trying to roll out the fifth-generation (5G) wireless network. This is set to deliver what is acknowledged to be unprecedented societal change on a global scale. We will have 'smart' homes, 'smart' businesses, 'smart' highways, 'smart' cities and self-driving cars. In addition to millions of new 5G base-stations on earth and 20,000 new satellites in space, 200 billion transmitting objects, according to estimates, will be part of the Internet of Things in 2020, and one trillion objects a few years later.

With each new generation of Wi-Fi that comes out, a new wave of health claims emerges – namely that human beings have never been exposed to this much of this type of radiation before – and scientists have not demonstrated that the proposed new infrastructure will not be harmful to us. 5G will result in a massive increase in inescapable, involuntary exposure to wireless radiation. Numerous independent scientists and researchers argue that there is experimental evidence of damage to DNA, cells and organ systems in a wide variety of plants and animals, and epidemiological evidence that the major diseases of modern civilisation – cancer, heart disease and diabetes – are in large part caused by electromagnetic pollution. It reminds me of the *Jurassic Park* clip where Dr Ian Malcolm says, 'Your scientists were so preoccupied with whether or not they could, that they didn't stop to think if they should.'

Does the AI lifestyle suit human beings?

According to some psychologists, happiness can be assessed with two simple questions. First, do you find meaning in your work? Second, do you have good relationships with those around you?

Our growing reliance on social technology rather than face-to-face interaction is thought to be making us feel more isolated. It means we feel less connected to others and our relationships are becoming more superficial and less rewarding. Modern life is making us lonelier – machines that give us abundance but leave us in want. Recent research indicates that this may be the next biggest public health issue, on a par with obesity and substance abuse.

In his TED talk, *What Makes a Good Life? Lessons from the Longest Study on Happiness,* Robert Waldinger reveals the answer is not power, status or achievement. The Grant Study, also known as the Harvard Study of Adult Development, is one of the most comprehensive longitudinal studies ever done. Researchers wanted to answer a seemingly simple question: what makes a good life? For 75 years, they tracked the lives of 724 men, year after year, asking about their work, their home lives and their health.

The study shows that social connections are really good for human beings, and that loneliness kills. It turns out that people who are more socially connected to family, friends and community are happier, physically healthier and longer-lived than those who are less well-connected. The experience of loneliness turns out to be toxic. People who are more isolated than they would like to be find that they are less happy, their health declines earlier in midlife, their brain functioning declines sooner and they live shorter lives than those who are not lonely. Some estimates put loneliness as increasing mortality risk by 26%. It turns out that meaningful connections are the oxygen of wellbeing.

All new inventions have a positive and a negative side. The gift of technology is to make everything we do better. I am a big believer in collective intelligence – the combination of human and artificial intelligence – for optimal decision-making. In radiology, for example, humans typically have 90% accuracy of detection. AI has an accuracy of 98%, but when used together they get to 99%, as both make different mistakes. AI is at its best when it is used to augment human decision-making – to improve rather than replace.

We should not be turning back the clock on technology. Such a conclusion by itself would be reductive. But there is a malign influence of big tech that we should be wary of. The more we subcontract our thinking, the more we render ourselves incapable of independent thought – until it becomes negligible.

> Dare to think for yourself.
> – KANT

To be human is not to be a robot

Technology promises a utopian future, but it is not a panacea that will save us. Take the burgeoning 'social credit' score that AI uses to define your place in Chinese society. Citizens who rank low are at risk of being banned from buying plane or train tickets, according to statements released by the country's National Development and Reform Commission. Visiting parents earns you points for virtuous behaviour, but if you then take away the value of honouring elders and ancestors, will that produce cynical behaviour? What does that mean for our society?

Automation confronts us with the most important question of all: what does being human mean? After 200,000 years, it seems we are still unprepared to tackle this most fundamental question.

Effective digital transformation requires a commitment to the power of the diverse perspective and an understanding of how human beings, and the human experience, will evolve as we become increasingly connected to the AI universe – a realm without barriers. The convergence of people and technology will define the future of work, but in the new paradigm of conscious leadership, the human element will always light the path forward. Otherwise, we are at risk of surrendering our moral responsibility.

This is a track that, once we go down it, seemingly becomes inevitable. Stephen Hawking warned that, unchecked, it could spell the end of the human race. Even Elon Musk admits that AI is capable of vastly more than we had imagined and that digital intelligence is a species-level risk. Ironically, the Chinese government seems to understand this. Its official policy is that AI is an existential risk to humanity if not developed properly.

The problem is that we do not know how to specify objectives correctly (perfectly). When a person states a given objective, there are usually associated, unstated, implicit underlying objectives or conditions to fulfilling that objective. The machine needs to understand that the objective is not fully formulated. 'I want a coffee' is not the sole objective. Otherwise we could happily run over people on our way to the store to get it. AI cannot think for humanity. Its picture completely excludes the soul.

Intelligence is what gives us power over other species. If we make something more intelligent than ourselves, it has more power than we do. Alan Turing, the founder of computer science, wrote, back in 1950, that eventually we can expect the machines to take control. We might be able to switch the power off at a strategic point, but as a species we will be humbled.

In a world being utterly reshaped by technology, people are hungrier than ever for a deeper and more authentic sense of our common humanity. If we can have a proper debate about these blind spots and about remaining in control, then this could herald a golden age for our species. Now is the time to bring in new bodies of law, legislative frameworks and regulatory paradigms to protect us and make digital safe for democracy.

Technology is a neutral medium – for now. It is not gender-biased – human beings are. Robots do not need to adjust their values – human beings do. We must prioritise the issues in our communities before sending humanity 230 million kilometres away to Mars. Certainly, it is clear that consumers would like to see these issues addressed.

Ethical Consumerism

> All labour that uplifts humanity has
> dignity and importance and should be
> undertaken with painstaking excellence.
> – MARTIN LUTHER KING JR

Post-capitalist positions

The unsustainable nature of corporate monopolies has become evident. Society charters businesses' right to operate. They can no longer be allowed to function in an indifferent, unengaged relationship with the society that gave them life in the first place.

As consumers, do we want Facebook to own Instagram, and WhatsApp too? Google to own YouTube and Waze? Amazon to own Whole Foods, Zappos and online advertising, as well as being an aspiring military behemoth? It is relentless – in fact, enter relentless.com into your web browser and you might be surprised what comes up.

Do we want the 'Big Four' to sell in consultancy services to the same companies that they audit – a clear conflict of interest? Sure, companies have detailed procurement and vendor management processes to promote competition, but when examined, they often serve to distract attention away from the cronyism that is inherent in many organisations.

The game of monopoly

As these companies have grown larger and more powerful, they have used their resources and control over the way we use the internet to squash small businesses and innovation. The corporate giants are known to structure their tax affairs to reduce what they pay. Apple was asked to fork out over €13 billion in back taxes after being granted 'illegal tax benefits' in Ireland; Amazon, ordered to pay €250 million in back taxes to Luxembourg; Facebook, punished with a €110 million fine for being opaque about its takeover of WhatsApp; chip-making company Qualcomm, fined €997 million for paying Apple to ensure that it would not buy chips from other companies.

In 2019, the Federal Trade Commission (FTC) voted to approve fining Facebook roughly $5 billion to settle an investigation into the company's privacy violations, the largest ever levied by the FTC against a technology company. It hardly mattered to investors and traders, who took Facebook's stock up by 1.8%, adding over $10 billion to Facebook's market cap.

Do not get me wrong; I have no ethical objection to companies getting rich – as long as it is not at the expense of other people. Five minutes after they get rich, their 'leaders' seem to pull up the ladder after themselves so that no one else does. In recent history, we have seen how the great innovators became monopolists. We saw it with the railroads and the oil barons, and now the tech giants. They took us past innovation to the making stage – and then onto the taking stage.

Where did all the small jobs go?

Small businesses are the engine of economic growth, and growth fuels prosperity for all. Over the years, we have witnessed the decimation of the British high street. The retail sector is in crisis owing to high costs, low levels of profitability and sales moving online. Thousands of high-street jobs are being lost as a result of high-profile retail administrations, and thousands more are at risk as other familiar names prepare for closure.

The resulting shift in labour markets is stark. A study looking at how the UK labour market had changed over the past decade found that the rise of online shopping had eliminated 289,000 'traditional' high-street roles. Eight out of ten of these entry-level retail jobs – positions like sales assistant and checkout operator – were held by women. The alternative jobs retail workers are getting are often low-paid and lead to working poverty. If insecure work continues to be a mainstay of the economy, we will need to boost the rights of these workers to ensure two-way flexibility.

The Royal Society for the Encouragement of Arts, Manufactures and Commerce (RSA) authored a review on the gig economy. Alan Lockey, who headed up the thinktank, said: 'The carnage on the high street has hollowed out many jobs traditionally held by women, but areas of growth related to e-commerce, such as van-driving, are going more to men. This is having a profound effect on individuals, families and society.'

Global shadow

Globalisation has brought immense benefits and lifted over two billion people out of poverty. It has also led multinational companies to be accused of social injustice and unfair working conditions, as well as a lack of concern for the environment, mismanagement of natural resources and ecological damage.

We have seen a rise of corporate power that has not been matched by corporate responsibility. Take a look at the fashion industry, predicated on objects having a short life. Fashion is known as capitalism's favourite child – a deregulated, short-term industry, high on resources, land, air and water, and based on a fad. In this industry, it is not uncommon to find men who have personal fortunes of billions presiding over female workers who earn 35 pence an hour in the Global South.

Fashion points us to the flaws in endless subcontracting, where everyone is trying to nickel-and-dime each other, while the people at the top get richer. Supply chains are intentionally multi-layered and multinational so that those at the top are less responsible for those at the bottom.

I could not believe my eyes when I went to Madagascar and saw the conditions of cobalt and nickel miners there. That experience confronts me with my own ethics, as I type on a device containing that product (with espoused values of 'environment' and 'supplier responsibility') – the technological equivalent of blood diamonds. As leaders, how do we know if our suppliers share our values? As consumers, at what point do we stop caring?

The true cost of a coffee

Coffee giants like Nespresso (owned by Nestlé) promise their beans are ethically sourced with zero-tolerance for child labour in their supply chains. Recently, the British Channel Four television show *Dispatches* aired video footage showing children in Guatemala lifting heavy loads in high temperatures, working up to seven days a week.

Of £2.50 spent on a typical cup of coffee on the high street, the shop receives 88p. Staff receive 63p, and 38p goes on tax. A profit of 25p goes to the coffee company. After other costs are accounted for, 10p is left for the coffee suppliers, of which 1p goes to the farmer, who uses only a fraction of this to pay coffee pickers.

In response, Nespresso has launched new TV commercials and created a six-step action plan including: doubling the number of Nespresso agronomists in Guatemala while hiring dedicated social workers before the harvest season; conducting more unannounced farm visits; improved documentation regarding the treatment of coffee pickers; expanding a pilot project to include 'child-friendly' spaces on coffee farms; increased education and outreach; and a hotline for reporting labour issues. If enforced, this goes a long way to achieving good working practices and fair treatment of workers, but fails to address the root cause – we need business models that provide decent wages to farmers and farm workers.

Trustworthiness over trust

In response to the *Dispatches* exposé, actor George Clooney – the face of the Nespresso brand – said, 'I was surprised and saddened to see this story.' In an age of celebrity and influencer marketing, it points to the importance of aligning values on all sides.

After revelations of influencers buying fake followers, hiring click farms and promoting products that they do not even use, consumer trust has eroded. Brands should be looking to eradicate nefarious practices throughout the digital ecosystem, and engage with their customers in authentic ways that inspire deeper trust.

Amber Atherton, CEO at Zyper, a community marketing platform, states:

Consumers are looking to engage with authentic people whose authentic product recommendations they can trust. What we're seeing is today's consumers, particularly Gen Z-ers, gravitating towards more grassroots communities, where people share information and original content about the brands and products they love with others they have a close relationship and something in common with. This is opening up new opportunities for brands to connect with existing customers who genuinely love their products by building strong online brand communities.

There is little to be said in favour of placing 'more trust' in anything or anyone, or in favour of 'restoring trust', unless we can distinguish well-directed from misdirected trust. Therefore, trustworthiness – the ability to be relied on as honest or truthful – matters more than trust.

Consumers making conscious choices

Ethical consumption is set to increase. The Co-op's Ethical Consumerism Report, which has tracked ethical expenditure in the UK over the past two decades, shows that the average spend on ethical purchases has grown fourfold in the past twenty years. The report – which focuses on various sectors of the economy, such as food, drinks, clothing, energy and eco-travel – highlights that back in 1999 the total size of the market was just £11.2 billion. Today, on a conservative basis, the figure is £41.1 billion.

The consumer is acting more and more like a committed citizen by getting informed and becoming involved. As we have seen, customers are seeking not only greater value but also greater meaning in the brands that they support. Consumers use brands and products to express their values. Companies that can cater to this extra dimension will have a crucial competitive advantage over firms that are fixated only on price and quality.

A report by Nielsen on Global Corporate Sustainability shows that globally 66% of consumers are ready to pay more for a good that comes from a responsible company. This indicator rises to 73% for millennials. Moreover, 81% of millennials expect their favourite brands to make open declarations about their purpose and public responsibility.

According to a Unilever consumer study, 33% of world consumers choose to buy from brands they consider to be doing social and environmental good. As much as 94% of Generation Z believe that companies should help to solve social and environmental issues. This generation, along with 'homelanders', consider their wallets to be the main way to become involved in CSR, with nine out of ten saying they will buy a product that has a social and/or environmental benefit.

What an incredible opportunity for businesses. The global natural cosmetics market size, as an example, is expected to reach a value of $48.04 billion by 2025, according to a report published by *Grand View Research, Inc.* High demand for natural health, 'green' or 'connected beauty' and wellness products is driving the growth, due to increasing awareness about the harmful impact of synthetic chemicals.

Re-visioning the circular economy
We cannot continue to pay lip service to the idea of change while our 'take, make, waste' model causes irreparable stress to the earth.

Disconnecting humanity from a dependence on natural-resource use will be key. The circular economy – which proposes to design, make, use and reuse products and services, to ensure they stay within the economy for as long as possible while minimising environmental harm – offers incredible potential and is gaining traction. A sustainable world does not mean a drop in the quality of life for consumers, and can be achieved without loss of revenue or extra costs for manufacturers.

I recommend leaders undertake the online B Impact Assessment, an impact management tool that helps companies assess their impact on various stakeholders, including their workers, community, customers and the environment, as well as best practices regarding governance. The free standardised tool can be used to compare their performance to thousands of other businesses and identify and track opportunities for improvement. They will receive two types of feedback. First, a snapshot provides a simple look at which of the 200 questions their company already excels at and which practices it could improve on. Then the comprehensive B Impact Report is a more holistic look at how a company scores across multiple questions related to the same impact topic, with no obligation to pursue certification.

Choosing to change

Governments are beginning to listen. In 2020, the 'doughnut' model of economics was formally adopted as the starting point for public policy decisions by the municipality of Amsterdam, the first city in the world to make such a commitment. The model, developed by British economist Kate Raworth, balances essential human needs and planetary boundaries.

The inner ring of the doughnut represents minimum standards of living, ranging from food and clean water to a certain level of housing, sanitation, energy, education, healthcare, gender equality, income and political voice. The outer ring of the doughnut represents the ecological limits of the planet. A big part of humanity's challenge is to get everyone out of the hole. Between the two rings is the sweet spot for humanity – the dough, where we meet the needs of all within the means of the planet.

Iceland is actively working through these issues too. The country wants to introduce a wellbeing economy, with GDP per head as one of thirty-nine indicators for social, economic and environmental progress. The indicators are linked to the UN Sustainable Development Goals (SDGs) and are based on official statistics to allow for international comparison. The prime minister is keen to develop the wellbeing economy pan-politically so that it endures beyond the four-year election cycle.

But ultimately it will be the consumer who gets to set the agenda. We have the power to demand dignified conditions for workers everywhere, with a fair living wage to enable communities to move out of poverty. It begs the question, what kind of a society do we want? Unchecked growth and Silicon Valley-style 'blitzscaled solutionism' or dignity, fairness and respect for all stakeholders, including the environment and future generations?

Consumer choice matters, as it reveals the values that are important to us. And with knowledge comes responsibility. We need an economy that is far more distributive by design, where value is shared and owned more equitably. There is an opportunity to create economies with far smaller, employee-owned, cooperatively owned, locally owned enterprises that are part of an ecosystem in which value is shared more equitably in the first place.

There is some interesting evidence suggesting that employees who own a stake in their business tend to be more engaged and productive. By widening ownership, we give more people a stake. This is not a new idea; according to the Employee Ownership Association, there are more than 100 UK companies with significant employee ownership – a section of the economy that is worth more than £25 billion annually. Greggs the Bakers has enjoyed much success by pushing out a share ownership model widely. In 2018, it bucked the trend of the British high-street slowdown, topping £1 billion in sales for the first time.

Every catastrophe is a new opportunity. If you look throughout history, the biggest and most necessary changes typically come in the wake of crises, much like our most important personal changes often come in the wake of our traumas.

If we are to retain a globalised system, we need to build institutions and capabilities that will ensure it functions in harmony with our principles. These only become real and active if they have an impact on our lives – usually to our cost. Perhaps in the future we will have to forgo the convenience of one-click ordering and walk to our local community shop instead. Increasing local resilience should surely be part of any new system, however global in reach.

Unfettered capitalism needs a moral boundary, where consumers can take the lead through a more conscious way of living. It will take a coalition of voices to achieve this strategic realignment, asking, 'Did it harm the environment? Could it be packaged more sustainably? Was there cruelty to animals? Is it cheap because of child slave labour?'

When billions of us make ethical choices, then we shift to a better world. Humanity has the power to move towards an inclusive, equitable and regenerative economic system, where we restore the balance of power in our democracy, promote competition and ensure that what is emerging can become a shared and lasting prosperity for all on earth.

After all, Mother Earth is a source of life, a home to us all, and not a mere resource.

Our Home

Compassion hurts. When you feel connected
to everything, you also feel responsible for
everything. And you cannot turn away.
– ANDREW BOYD

The ecological divide is a disconnect between self, business
and nature that shows up in many forms of environmental
destruction, of resource scarcity, falling water tables, climate
change and soil erosion. And if you want to put a number on the
ecological divide, the number is 1.5. Latterly, we have been operating a world economy that uses 1.5 times the regenerational capacity
of our home. Our choices are now coming home to roost.

Some have characterised the human species as enemies of the
earth. I have a different perspective. I believe we have forgotten that
we *are* the earth.

We are one earth, but as we did not take care of ourselves, we
lived as though the earth was an inexhaustible source of our supposed needs.

I used to know that we were inseparable from nature only at a rational level. That was until a family in Tibet extended to me the honour of attending a sky burial. For Buddhists in Tibet, offering the bodies to vultures or other birds is the last great and honourable thing to do. It is an offering of generosity back to the earth that gave them life. It was on a mountain at 15,000 feet that I truly understood that the earth nourishes us, just as we nourish it. Like leaves that fall, we eventually go back into earth, taking and leaving nothing except our legacy.

Unification

Unresolved conflicts of the past have created a world mapped out into borders of coloured lines and blocked out lands that make human beings believe in separation. The memory of this map with the countries that our one unified race has invented encouraged us to compete for resources and habituated us to the curse of war.

This man-made illusion of fragmented geography was then applied to the water of planet earth, by teaching different names for spaces covered by water. Not only did we cut it with different words like ocean or sea, but we attributed names to those invented parts. We then applied laws to those parts, permitting some to be polluted and some to be preserved.

The ultimate truth is that water is one unified being that we all live inside. It is like one giant drop with different states. When water freezes we call it an iceberg, when it fills a hole or valley we say lakes and rivers. We call it clouds, rain, steam, mist, ice, waterfalls, the liquid that makes plants grow, that makes ships float, allows fish to swim, that we build bridges over, transverse with highways and damn to create hydropower. The same water is used to make health-giving treatments and water our crops with pesticides. We use the same great stream of water to clean our factories and rinse our personal waste, and the water is then returned to that stream and passed back to our taps, used to shower our bodies and create our morning drinks of water, coffee and tea. When we dig into the earth we believe we have created a well. Those who build toxic factories build them far from where they sail and swim, thinking it is different water. And those who dispose of the toxins deliver them to the seas of other lands, believing that other seas exist

Anything that we give to water will be returned back to all life somewhere. We are now called upon to elevate our perspective and realise that water is a being that supports all life on earth. It flows everywhere, from the top of the world to our homes – underneath, inside, outside, above, below; as we breathe it and drink it, it passes through us and becomes us. Life on this planet is a shared experience of living creatures inhabiting the same sphere of earth, fuelled by living inside the various states of water.

But human beings, educated in fragmentation, are attempting to deal with the future of earth without realising the errors of perception expressed in our languages. We distract ourselves from recognising that the damage we cause is due to the human lack of understanding of the co-dependence of life, and that the bodies we inhabit are being harmed by this same lack of awareness.

We are capable of experiencing and understanding our life on this planet in a new and fresh way, seeing ourselves as we have never seen ourselves before. Now is the time to free human perception by sharing this vision of the unification of nature, so that we may act with more intelligence based on true wisdom. After all, our species' name, *Homo sapiens,* is from the Latin for 'wise' ones.

Taking care of the future now

The scale of the challenge certainly seems overwhelming. But still, the best way to take care of the future is to take care of the present moment.

Because if I look after me, then I look after you, and I look after the earth.

Underlying the change is a critical need for the political will to undertake large-scale reform. This is particularly true in light of creating an enabling environment for investment and participation by the private sector. Imagine a world where business puts partnership at the heart of what it does all the time, not just on specific issues (e.g. palm oil sourcing), but also on systemic change (e.g. the global food system).

If we are to accept that we live in a world of global interdependence, we must also accept the sharing of responsibility that comes with it. As an example, the Great Green Wall project is an $8 billion plan to reforest 247 million acres of degraded land across the width of Africa, stretching from Dakar to Djibouti, spearheaded by the African Union and funded by the World Bank, the European Union and the United Nations. It was launched in 2007 to halt the expansion of the Sahara by planting a barrier of trees running 4,815 miles along its southern edge. The goal is to transform the lives of millions living on the front line of climate change by restoring agricultural land ruined by decades of overuse. When the project is completed, it should provide food, stem conflict and discourage migration.

In the UK, a 'Northern Forest' is transforming the landscape of northern England. Fifty million trees will be planted around the cities of Liverpool, Manchester, Leeds, Sheffield and Hull over the next twenty-five years by the Woodland Trust and its partners. Collectively, these will go a long way to help beleaguered populations of insects, pine martens, red squirrels and other vulnerable creatures, providing habitats for dozens of animals that have been badly hit by pesticides and habitat loss. The project will benefit 13 million people and generate social, economic and environmental benefits worth an estimated £2.5 billion.

The Business Roundtable recently released a new *Statement on the Purpose of a Corporation* signed by nearly 200 chief executive officers, and the World Economic Forum launched a new Davos Manifesto to tackle today's environmental and social challenges. We all stand to gain from more resilient communities, reliable access to natural resources, and an educated and healthy population to support the global workforce. Companies need to focus on causes that are integral to their business, searching for ways to contribute. Our approach should be forward- and outward-looking, recognising the interconnectedness of everything and everyone.

Increasingly, the 17 SDGs and 169 specific sub-goals are defining the agenda for inclusive economic growth through to 2030. The SDGs were created collaboratively by 193 governments to address some of the world's toughest challenges and most pertinent problems. They cover the issues that require companies to rethink their approaches to value generation, but are not just for global governments or large corporations to tackle – they empower citizens, entrepreneurs, leaders, employees and activists to collaborate under a common language and intention.

The goals are:

1. **No poverty**
2. **Zero hunger**
3. **Good health and wellbeing**
4. **Quality education**
5. **Gender equality**
6. **Clean water and sanitation**

7.   **Affordable and clean energy**
8.   **Decent work and economic growth**
9.   **Industry, innovation and infrastructure**
10. **Reduced inequalities**
11. **Sustainable cities and communities**
12. **Responsible consumption and production**
13. **Climate action**
14. **Life below water**
15. **Life on land**
16. **Peace, justice and strong institutions**
17. **Partnerships for the goals**

Which of the goals speak to you, giving you the energy of aspiration and action?

Nature is the real treasure

Following the prehistoric breakup of the supercontinent Gondwana, Madagascar split from the Indian subcontinent around 88 million years ago, allowing native plants and animals to evolve in relative isolation and thus creating a biodiversity hotspot. Over 90% of its wildlife is found nowhere else on earth, and it is presently under threat from deforestation and habitat destruction, agricultural fires, erosion, soil degradation and overexploitation of living resources.

There is a beautiful reserve in Madagascar called Vohimana, where nature and humanity coexist in harmony. I had lent my support remotely, so I was overjoyed when I was given the opportunity to visit and spend some time in the verdant green forests there. On my adventure, I discovered the plants that help us look young, those that create scents for our perfumes and the ones being researched to cure cancers – most of them endemic and in danger of going extinct if we do not protect them.

At night, I was fortunate to spot a fat-tailed dwarf lemur, a mammal much cuter than its name would suggest. This particular species hibernates for up to seven months a year, and is critical for research into suspended animation. This tiny creature in Madagascar could even hold the key for humanity to travel through space. Sadly, lemurs are now considered the most endangered group of animals on the planet.

Described as the lungs of the planet, the Amazon rainforest produces roughly a fifth of the earth's oxygen (one breath in five) and more than two-fifths of all the species in the world live there. Deforestation is up 88% and man-made fires in the Amazon are destroying the rainforest at a rate of 1.5 football fields per minute.

But there is hope in the form of the indigenous people. Where they are, there is no deforestation. These local communities ensure that biodiversity and the environment are protected. In the new paradigm, we must turn towards them as frontline guardians of the environment. Indigenous peoples make up 4% of the global population and they protect 80% of the world's biodiversity on their land. The elders know how to protect their communities and will help the rest of humanity make the eco shift in the coming ecological age.

The earth has existed for over four and a half billion years – 22,500 times longer than humanity. Over the course of history, more than 99% of species that ever existed have gone extinct. We are reminded of our oneness in global pandemics, which strike at us all, regardless of race, religion, political views, nationality, borders, age, status or wealth. All of humanity is equally vulnerable, from the homeless to royalty. This is the ultimate reminder that we are inextricably connected to each other. And whatever happens to the earth, happens to us.

Humanity now has the opportunity to wake up and examine our relationship with ourselves, each other and our home, Mother Earth.

In Hawaii, to be 'pono' means to be in a state of harmony or balance with oneself, others, the land, work and life itself. If you are living a life that is based on pono, you live in a way that seeks to improve the world around you. Working towards a pono life is not an idealistic, 'change the world overnight' attitude. It is a guiding principle that precedes an action. A common question asked to children is, 'Is it pono?' In other words, 'Do your actions reflect bringing more harmony and good into the world?' The state of Hawaii's motto is 'Ua Mau ke Ea o ka Aina i ka Pono', meaning 'The life of the land is perpetuated in righteousness'.

Science is never truly 'settled'

Human bodies are themselves communities of cooperation whose genetic material consists primarily of the genes of the trillions of microorganisms that form the microbiota that keep us alive. In other words, we emerge from cooperative systems – in fact, we *are* cooperative systems. We are already connected; the question is, how does humanity consciously move into connection?

> A human being is part of the whole called by us the 'Universe', a part limited in time and space. We experience ourselves, our thoughts and feelings, as something separate from the rest. A kind of optical delusion of consciousness. This delusion is a kind of prison for us, restricting us to our personal desires and to affection for a few persons nearest to us. Our task must be to free ourselves from the prison by widening our circle of compassion to embrace all living creatures and the whole of nature in its beauty. ... The true value of a human being is determined primarily by the measure and the sense in which they have obtained liberation from the self. ... We shall require a substantially new manner of thinking if humanity is to survive.
> – ALBERT EINSTEIN

We are connected by invisible threads. It was not so long ago that physicists made the astonishing discovery that the perceived separation of electrons does not actually mean they are separate. If two electrons have been paired, they continue to operate as an entangled whole even if the distance between them is the vastness of space. If the spin of one electron is changed, its pair changes instantly, faster than the speed of light.

When scientists set out to assemble the first complete human genome, which was a composite of several individuals, they deliberately gathered samples from people who self-identified as members of different races. In June 2000, when the results were announced at a White House ceremony, Craig Venter, a pioneer of DNA sequencing, observed, 'The concept of race has no genetic or scientific basis.'

We are not separate from each other. There really is only one race – the human race.

Astronauts have often told us that when they go into space, something strange happens to them. They cannot stop staring back at our planet. They called it 'earth-gazing'. Seeing earth in its entirety somehow did not make astronauts feel insignificant, but gave them a feeling of increased connection, awe and care:

> From the moon, the Earth is so small and so fragile, and such a precious little spot in that universe, that you can block it out with your thumb. Then you realise that on that spot, that little blue and white thing, is everything that means anything to you – all of history and music and poetry and art and death and birth and love, tears, joy, games, all of it right there on that little spot that you can cover with your thumb. And you realise from that perspective that you've changed forever, that there is something new there, that the relationship is no longer what it was.
>
> – RUSTY SCHWEICKART

In the '60s, Rusty Schweickart's journey into space went so smoothly that for the last two or three days of the mission he spent most of his time just looking out of the window of the spacecraft, earth-gazing. It was ten years before he told anyone what happened to him in those days, as he could not even figure out how to do it. Eventually, he gave a talk at the Lindisfarne Association and had a flash of insight that he would describe what happened to him in the second person and in the present tense.

He asked people to imagine that they were sitting in his body:

Imagine I'm not me, but I'm a sensory apparatus of humanity. So yes, my eyes are seeing, my senses are feeling, but you're feeling too. You see the western coast of the Americas. You're looking for what's familiar to you. You live in Houston, so you notice when you go over Texas. And then now you're going over Florida, and you know that place. That's what you've been doing now for several days; you've been looking for the places that are familiar.

But now you notice that something has shifted. Now you're looking forward to seeing the Sinai Peninsula. And now you're looking forward to seeing the western coast of India. And you realise slowly that you're looking forward to seeing all these places that you didn't grow up with. You now realise that your identity has shifted, and you're now identifying with all of it.

And now you're in the last day. You've now shifted that identity. You've been going over all these places, which are now equally appreciated. You feel the same connection. You feel the same love you felt just for the place you knew. One human family as a planetary whole.

Now you're drifting over what we call the Middle East. You see that stretch of division between the Mediterranean Sea and the land. And you see the familiar outline of the Dead Sea, and you see the desert. You're staring down at this, and for the first time you realise that there are no lines. Every time you've ever seen this before, it has been a map. Every time you've ever seen that familiar geography, there have been lines drawn. Of course, the lines move with history. You realise in this instant of awakening, there are no lines. And you realise, right now, people are killing each other over lines and belief systems which do not actually exist except in their imagination.

Several years after his talk at Lindisfarne, Rusty was asked, 'So, Rusty, if you looked at all of that right now, all these years later, what did you actually see when you were up there?' He paused. He just sat there with his eyes closed and replied, 'I saw a baby about to be born.'

I do not think any of us know what is coming, but it could be quite wonderful.

Part Three — The Awakened Future

From Ego to True Self

And you? When will you begin that
long journey into yourself?
– Rumi

For many, the sense of self is ego-based. Individual egos have self-centred aims, tastes, desires, opinions, likes or dislikes. The very construct of the ego brings with it a built-in conflict with other egos. If you think about it, it is surprising that separate egos, each with their own set of rules and agendas, ever get together in the first place. When they do, their connections always risk unravelling because each ego is primarily tied to what it wants.

The egoic self starts out needing the illusion of protection by clinging to externals like money, status, the bonds of relationships, developing a fit body. These are good things on their own, but they are not so good when they reinforce the attitude of 'us versus them'.

In Trina Paulus's book, *Hope for the Flowers*, two caterpillars get caught up in the long-held fallacy of competition and struggle to reach the top of a 'caterpillar pillar'. By their journey's end, they learn that their true nature, and that of every other caterpillar, is not one of winning and being at the top, but of going within and emerging as beautiful butterflies, born to soar. Like the caterpillars in that tale, early on in our lives we may receive messages that we must compete in order to succeed, whether it be in sports, tests at school or finding a job. There seemingly must be winners and losers; those who stand out above the rest and those who are left behind. These scenarios give a sense that there is deep lack in the world, with only so much glory, money and other resources to go around. This perspective can create such urgency to be seen to be the best that we may be willing to do whatever it takes to win or be right, even if it is out of alignment with our values. We may begin to see the success of others as a threat, as if there is not enough room for everyone to win.

To survive, the ego has to believe it is real and that it is separate. It does not want to change or be changed, despite its sufferings and fears. It clings to being 'right' at any cost. This seems to occur in part because we see opposing facts as undermining our sense of identity – but that is the ego self, not the true self. If we can be at peace with people who have different views from our own, then the fault lines will disappear.

Ego or authentic self?

> The true self grows in inverse proportion
> to the growth of egoism.
> – TEILHARD DE CHARDIN

Everything in life begins with connection. In each moment, we are choosing to join or separate – to connect or disconnect.

What makes relationships challenging often comes down to one factor: we build the relationship from the outside in, believing something we want is not happening because of someone else – who is outside us. We must learn to connect first with ourselves and create a relationship from the inside out. The first rule of building heart-to-heart connections is that even though it takes two people to create a relationship, the responsibility for connecting starts with you. The second rule is that everything depends on your level of awareness.

It can be hard uncovering who we really are from our thinking mind alone, as we so often identify with our egos or our inauthentic selves.

Neuroscientist Dr James Hardt offers us some red flags that indicate that the ego mind is in charge:

- Feeling anxious or worried
- Creating doubt about our decisions
- Thinking rigidly, not creatively
- Wanting to impress others
- Saying or doing things we regret
- Having low expectations of ourselves and our lives
- Hiding or denying our true feelings
- Feeling like a victim of life's circumstances
- Getting trapped in endless mind chatter, mostly negative

The following characteristics are more prevalent in the true self:

- Feeling optimistic most of the time
- Experiencing trust
- Going with the flow and being open to change

- Being able to accept oneself without judgement
- Taking responsibility for actions and decisions
- Not projecting feelings onto others or blaming others
- Knowing how to accept and how to receive
- Listening to and acknowledging feelings
- Knowing how to ask for help

The choice is ours

From an ego perspective, we are just one person – an isolated speck standing against immense outside forces. I have survived bullying, abuse and being diagnosed with an autoimmune disease at the age of 24. So much pain in my life – emotional and physical. In fact, there is not a moment in my day that I am not in physical pain, as the bones in my spine fuse together.

My condition is worst when I am inactive. When I wake every morning and cannot move, I am grateful for the opportunity to choose my attitude. Viktor Frankl, a Jewish psychiatrist who suffered greatly during the Holocaust of the Second World War, said that the last of human freedoms is the ability to choose one's attitude in a given set of circumstances. Between stimulus and response there is a space, and in that space is our power to choose our response. In our response lies our growth and our freedom. I get the chance to choose growth and joy every single day.

My journey has taken me from blame and spitefulness to oneness and unconditional love. After years of being stuck, I found the only way to break through was through forgiveness. There were some people I needed to forgive, and others whose forgiveness I sought. Reaching out to people from my past and seeking their forgiveness – regardless of who did what – was like throwing away heavy bags that had been weighing me down for many years.

> Through an illness, accident, loss, or fright, one
> way or another, we are all faced with incidents
> that teach us how to become less selfish and
> judgemental, and more compassionate and
> generous. Yet some of us learn the lesson and
> manage to become milder, while others end
> up becoming even harsher than before. The
> only way to get closer to Truth is to expand
> your heart so that it will encompass all
> humanity and still have room for more Love.
> – ELIF SHAFAK, *THE FORTY RULES OF LOVE*

Dr Jane Goodall tells of pumpkin farmers in Africa who had a problem with monkeys destroying their crops. The farmers decided to put a hole in the top of the pumpkin, just big enough for a monkey's hand to go through. The monkeys could get their hand inside, but when they clenched their fist to grab the food, they became 'trapped'. The farmers would then capture the monkeys. It didn't occur to the animals that if they let go of the seeds they would be able to get away. It really is that simple. All we need to do is let go, because, like the monkeys, the truth is we are not trapped.

Forgiveness does not mean you condone a behaviour or make a wrong into a right. It simply means you give yourself permission to accept and release what was done.

Did you know that a peacock's feathers are made by the bird eating thorns? What a beautiful image, that the harsh things we have to digest can contribute to our beauty. I have come to learn that what happens *to* us, happens *for* us.

We are all doing the best we can from our current level of consciousness. Said differently, we are each on our own journey, and we have to meet people where they are at. The truth is, if you are holding on to a grudge, that grudge is also holding on to you. Not forgiving someone does not give you power – it actually takes your power away. Forgiveness is not something you do for the person who wronged you; it is something you do for yourself.

Relationships begin with being at peace with yourself – having a connection with yourself that nothing can break from the outside. Other people become a reflection of the loving, kind, peaceful relationship you have with yourself. You cannot receive what you cannot give.

The scenery out there reflects the situation in here.

We can choose to connect with another person or not, but we cannot choose to disconnect from ourselves. Many people are uncomfortable with this truth, spending vast amounts of time trying to escape from themselves with all kinds of activities, work and distractions. Working from the outside in will fall short of the ideal, and lead to frustration, conflict and lack of fulfilment in the end.

Removing the ego's old toys

The ego – the part of ourselves always looking to protect itself – can only pretend to be compassionate. Deep down it wants something in return, such as admiration or submission. But when you take time to look at people in the light of true compassion, everything can change. Powerful forces come into play when you stop to ask, 'What do I really know about this person? I may see them every day, but do I know what makes them cry, what keeps them from sleeping, what their home situation is?' It is as simple as pausing before you speak and asking yourself, 'Is it true? Is it kind? Is it necessary?' If you can accept that people are doing the best they can from their level of consciousness, you no longer need to judge. Besides, the people who need the most love often show it in the least loving way.

When our inner strength gets activated, we realise it was never really us against the world. The truth is, abundance exists all around – in nature, in the love of our friends and families. In going within and connecting with our true selves, we find it easier to understand this and appreciate what we already have. We no longer exist in competition with our fellow human beings, choosing instead to see the world as a place where every one of us can express our unique talents and succeed. But we cannot be compassionate to others if we are not compassionate towards ourselves. We are all enough as we are, and we are all meant to be here, being what we are, fulfilling our own roles and destinies.

The answers really do lie within

The lens through which we see the world changes when we practise gratitude every day. It sounds simple, but when we go through the day staying conscious about what we are grateful for, our paradigm shifts. In a group of people who wake up every morning and note down three things they are grateful for (they have to be new each day), those who were testing as low-level pessimists will test as low-level optimists after 21 consecutive days. It sounds small, but here is the amazing thing. Harvard researcher Shawn Achor says we can do this with 84 year olds who have genes for pessimism. If you can do this for 21 days, then even if you have practised pessimism for eight decades of your life – even if you were born with genes for pessimism – two minutes could trump your genes and environment.

> Gratitude is not only the greatest of
> virtues, but the parent of all the others.
> – CICERO

The true self is a state of awareness, not a thing, mood, sensation or feeling. All it takes is a shift in awareness to discover that love, peace and lack of conflict exist inside us and have the power to change any situation. And awareness always precedes change.

Harvard brain scientist Dr Jill Bolte Taylor experienced the power of collective energy when she suffered a devastating haemorrhagic stroke that wiped out the function of much of her brain. With no memory or language recognition, she became acutely aware of the energy surrounding her as she embarked on her long road to recovery. The request Jill made of every person who came into contact with her throughout her recovery was, 'Please take responsibility for the energy you bring into this space.' Each one of us holds the power to transform our collective consciousness.

We all have a role to play

Opposites do not exist in reality. Let us take the seeming opposites of light and dark. There is no such thing as darkness; there is only light. The conditions can be described as 'light is either present or not' or 'light is present at varying degrees'. Thus, there is only one variable: the presence or absence of light. That means that the opposite of good is not evil; it is merely the absence of good.

I used to be dogmatic about the wrongness of the nepotism, bigotry, abuse and corruption I witnessed in the world. Of course, the triggers had something to latch on to, given my backstory. This was perhaps my greatest hurdle, keeping me stuck on my journey for many years. But this is where the systemic principle of acknowledgement comes in. I have come to learn that the propensity to either/or-ness condemns human consciousness by reinforcing the dilemma of the opposites and the false duality of perception.

When your perceptions shift, your personal story shifts too. Most people have their telescopes turned outwards; they are waiting for better scenery to show up, populated by nicer people and possessions. Inside yourself is the control switch to any perception. Turn the telescope around and you will realise that things become better because of you, not because of externals. At any given moment when you apply a negative tag to your experience, you are missing an opportunity to unburden yourself.

Allowing more of our innate goodness to emanate out into the world draws abundance within and without. When we choose actions that bring happiness and success to others, the fruit of our karma is happiness and success. The secret to success is to choose one value and pursue it with intensity. One could choose kindness, compassion, forgiveness, understanding or noncritical acceptance. It is the wish to bring happiness to others, to brighten their day and lighten their load – simply to be friendly and complimentary to everyone one meets in the course of a day.

Human beings are limitless, and yet we are limited. The better we understand the true nature of humanity, the better we can move within ourselves and the world.

Winning the Mind Game

The intuitive mind is a sacred gift and
the rational mind is a faithful servant. We
have created a society that honours the
servant and has forgotten the gift.
– ALBERT EINSTEIN

Reclaiming the full power of your mind

When everything is flowing in our idea of how we think things
should be, it is easy to think we are living in harmony with the
rhythms of the universe. But when there is a gap between what we
want and how our life is unfolding, we are more likely to feel stress
and doubt. We may judge a situation as wrong or unfair, or judge
ourselves for what we perceive as shortcomings or failures. When
our mind is filled with resistance, it is hard to access our innate sense
of wisdom, clarity and creativity. We get caught up in our thoughts
and begin to think we are our thoughts.

At some stage in our lives, we all have doubts, be it about our abilities at work or whether we deserve to be loved for who we truly are. Our mind is so powerful that if we hold in mind a single thought, such as, 'My relationships never work out,' then that is most likely going to happen. Our unconscious genie, which can only take orders and not make decisions, sees to it that our relationships do not work out. This is a basic law of consciousness – we are subject only to what we hold in our mind. The mind controls the brain, which acts as a receiving station, like a radio. Put simply, we are free to choose whether or not to buy into a negative belief system.

Breaking the mind control

For negativity to apply to our life, we must first subscribe to it and then give it the energy of belief. How does this apply to everyday life? Dr David Hawkins offers the following example. Say the media reports unemployment is at a record high and the news anchor says, 'No jobs are available.' At this point, we are free to refuse to buy into the negative thought form. We can say instead, 'Unemployment does not apply to me.' Words have power. By our refusing to accept the negative belief, we do not allow it to have a hold over us.

Napoleon Hill, the 20th-century pioneer of positive thinking, once observed that, 'The subconscious mind makes no distinction between constructive and destructive thought impulses. It works with the material we feed it, through our thought impulses. The subconscious mind will translate into reality a thought driven by fear, just as readily as it will translate into reality a thought driven by courage or faith.'

We teach our subconscious everything it knows. If we subscribe to negative thoughts without challenging them, we run the risk of storing them in our subconscious as reality. The next time a negative thought enters your mind, ask yourself, 'Says who?' It will help you reconnect to your authentic self and the truth of the situation. And just breathe. After all, the nostrils are the remote control to the brain.

Thoughts are like goldfish in a bowl; the real Self is the space between the thoughts, or more precisely, the field of silent awareness underneath all thoughts. If we acknowledge the presence of such thoughts and impulses, and recognise that they are not us, but mere waves that pass through our inner space, they become quiet. Once they are quiet, they no longer unconsciously run us.

I have come to learn that any given situation in itself is distinct from my response or reaction to it. When we recognise this, the challenge the situation represents can no longer take control like a puppet master, directing our reactions. I have discovered that when we pause, accept each moment and actively take responsibility for how we choose to respond (note the true meaning of that word, and its difference from the knee-jerk of 'reaction'), the pressure of a difficult moment gets diffused. We control our actions, and therefore we control the outcomes. That, to me, is mindfulness. And the action of returning to the moment of now can be practised anywhere, anytime.

Imagine two people who arrive at the airport to discover that their flight has been cancelled. One accepts the news with a sigh, goes to the bookstore and gets immersed in a fascinating book. The other grumbles, yells at the check-in agent and paces up and down, seething with anger. The same event produces a different outcome in the two people. This is important to realise, because without being able to instantly produce a jet to take them where they want to go, they can nonetheless create a positive moment simply through the power of awareness.

By escaping old patterns and conditioning, we can become the agents of change. In fact, our awareness *is* the change. Return now to the airport and the cancelled flight. At any one moment the angry passenger could have said, 'This is me choosing to get angry about a situation that I can't change. The choice is mine.' When we face a crisis, challenge or setback, Deepak Chopra reminds us to tell ourselves: 'This is me reacting – the situation itself is a blank canvas – it has no specific meaning until I choose to give it one.'

When we accept where we are without judgement, we start to weaken the attachment our mind has to its thoughts. This is how we win the mind game and become centred, engaged and receptive. We are in the present, which is the most important moment of our lives. From here, we are free to create any response we desire, and from there, any outer reflection is possible.

Expanding the mind

In 2016, I visited the Manhattan bar at the Regent Hotel in Singapore for a nightcap before retiring to my hotel room. It was late and only three people sat on stools near the bar. As I tucked into a bowl of truffle popcorn, a gentleman turned to me and said, 'I have a message for you.' I avoided the temptation to run away. Through conversation he told me, 'You need to go to the Biocybernaut Institute.' I had no idea what this was, but somehow I felt compelled to agree to go there. Two years later, I found myself on a plane heading to Bavaria to attend the mysterious Biocybernaut neurofeedback brainwave training.

Brainwaves are the electrical impulses produced as our brain cells communicate with one another. They are produced by synchronised electrical pulses from masses of neurons communicating with each other, and they tell us a great deal about how we feel and function – our thought habits, stress levels, underlying mood and overall brain function.

Every experience we have as a human being is because we have an underlying pattern of brainwaves, the study of which forms a vast area of research. The *Brainworks* definitions below give us a basic idea.

Delta waves

These are the slowest of all brainwaves (0.5–4 Hz), and are generated in deepest meditation and dreamless sleep. Delta waves suspend external awareness and are the source of empathy. This is the state where healing and rejuvenation are stimulated, which is why it is so crucial to get enough sleep each night.

Theta waves

Theta brainwaves (4–8 Hz) are dominant in deep meditation. Theta is our gateway to learning, memory and intuition. In theta, our senses are withdrawn from the external world and focused on signals originating from within. It is that twilight state which we normally only experience fleetingly as we wake or drift off to sleep. It is where we hold our 'stuff' – our fears, troubled history and nightmares.

Alpha waves

Alpha brainwaves (8–13 Hz) are dominant during quietly flowing thoughts and in some meditative states. Alpha is 'the power of now', being here, in the present. Alpha is the resting state for the brain. Alpha waves aid overall mental coordination, calmness, alertness, mind/body integration and learning.

Beta waves

Beta brainwaves (13–32 Hz) dominate our normal waking state of consciousness when attention is directed towards cognitive tasks. Beta is a 'fast' activity, present when we are alert and attentive, engaged in problem-solving, judgement, decision-making or focused mental activity. Continual high-frequency processing is not a very efficient way to run the brain, as it takes a great deal of energy.

Gamma waves

The mind has to be quiet to access gamma, the most subtle of the brainwave frequencies (32–100 Hz). Gamma was dismissed as 'spare brain noise' until researchers discovered it was highly active when in states of universal love, altruism and the 'higher virtues'. Gamma is also above the frequency of neuronal firing, so how it is generated remains a mystery. It is speculated that gamma rhythms modulate perception and consciousness, and that a greater presence of gamma relates to expanded consciousness and spiritual emergence.

Brainwave training

Studies have shown that brainwave neurofeedback training results in significant reductions in depression, fatigue, tension, anger, anxiety and hostility. Stanford Research Institute scientists who did the training reported an average of 50% increase in creativity. Another study measured the brainwaves of beginners, intermediate and advanced Zen meditators. The brainwaves of neurofeedback trainees were compared to the brainwaves of Zen meditators at each level of experience. Brainwave patterns found only in Zen meditators with 21–40 years of meditation experience were found in participants after seven days of alpha brainwave training. Furthermore, evidence shows a +11.7 point increase in IQ that remains stable 12 months out.

Neurofeedback operates on the principle that you can become aware of which state, or band of activity, your brain is in, and then consciously shift from one to another. The training gives alpha feedback on the left and right occipitals and the left and right centrals, and also gives feedback on the coherence between left and right hemispheres of the brain.

Essentially, neurofeedback training helps to quieten the mind. Thinking hard (beta activity) does not usually result in flashes of brilliant creativity; nor does it lead to emotional states of being that nurture our body and soul. Not thinking – not having that barrage of words marching through your mind – actually leads to healthier brainwave states, which link us to our deep wellsprings of creativity and to the unconscious mind.

The Biocybernaut training was intense; over 12 hours a day, with periods attached to EEG electrodes in soundproof and light-proof rooms. The real-time immediate feedback on alpha in the form of musical tones encourages the production of more alpha waves. Increases in alpha activity are correlated with increases in self-actualising values, inner directedness, spontaneity, self-regard and self-acceptance. In brief, alpha puts you into an enhanced state of awareness. When the alpha waves get bigger in amplitude, the tones become louder. The feedback, coupled with the intention to make more alpha waves, encourages the brain to make more of the brainwaves that have just triggered the feedback, and allows brain-waves to organise, grow and synchronise across the head.

The training also taught me how to access theta, shifting from using my conscious processor at twenty thousand bits per second to using my unconscious processor, which processes information at four billion bits per second. To access theta brainwaves, I would recline in an armchair to promote access to the 'hypnagogic' state between waking and sleep. By learning to use a conscious theta brainwave pattern, we can access and more effectively influence the powerful subconscious part of ourselves that is normally inacces-sible to our waking mind. While in a theta state, the mind is capable of deep and profound learning, healing and growth.

I experienced profound insights in the chamber. As the tones became longer, more frequent and louder, the real-time feedback indicated that my brainwaves were organising, growing and syn-chronising across my head. Thus I could ask myself, 'Who am I? What am I here for? How can I best serve humanity?'

I came to realise that the subconscious has the answers to all our problems and influences what happens to us on a conscious level. The subconscious never rests. In fact, many of the world's most successful people intentionally direct the workings of their subconscious mind while they are sleeping. That is how Thomas Edison is said to have invented the light bulb.

Awakening your sleeping genius

You can try to direct your subconscious mind to create the outcomes you seek by unlocking connections and solutions to your problems and projects. Take a few moments before you go to bed to focus on the things you are trying to accomplish. Ask yourself, 'What do I need to know?' and while you are asleep, your subconscious mind will get to work.

> Never go to sleep without a request
> to your subconscious.
> – THOMAS EDISON

First thing in the morning, when your creative brain is most attuned, write down whatever comes to mind. Mental creation always precedes physical creation. Your thoughts are the blueprint of the life you are building, and when you learn to channel your thinking – both consciously and subconsciously – you create the conditions that make the achievement of your goals inevitable.

Interpreting the EEG of my brainwaves, the team of scientists discovered that I had tremendously high-amplitude, low-frequency, organised delta in a waking state. Thus I had experiences beyond my everyday physical reality, and overcame any sense of separation from other people, which was replaced by a profound and undeniable awareness of the oneness that unites us all at the deeper levels of reality.

Of central importance was learning to practise forgiveness and gratitude. On my last day in the chamber, I decided to honour the gentleman from the bar in Singapore. Flooded in alpha, I suddenly remembered his business card flashing in front of me and saw his name and email address in my mind's eye. How incredible our brains are when we escape the busy, thinking mind. I sent him an email later that evening: 'You won't remember me, but you gave me a message a couple of years ago in a bar in Singapore that profoundly changed my life.' Half an hour later a reply came through. 'Of course I remember you, Samie. I have just arrived in Bavaria.'

Using higher mind states to see the silver lining

When we become quiet, more observant, more contemplative and less reactive, we become able to find the gift buried in every problem awaiting us. As our awareness expands, we connect with our higher self and begin to see the hidden possibilities in whatever challenge we are facing. With a shift of perception, we realise that what appeared to be a devastating setback has actually cleared the way for our rebirth and transformation. From the soul's perspective there is no such thing as success or failure, there is only the present moment, which is filled with infinite possibilities.

> Doing nothing often leads to the
> very best of something.
> – WINNIE THE POOH

The key to creating the life that you want and deserve is to be fully aware and fully present in all that you do every day. Stay aware of your moment-to-moment choices and choose with intention, knowing that every thought, feeling, belief and action is creating your reality.

We are now in the now

The quiet mind liberates us from the endless treadmill of repeating thoughts and takes us to a state of constant alertness, where we are watchful of what comes into the mind, moment to moment, and thus of how to respond to such promptings.

Life is perfectly arranged to bring us to the now of every moment. Regardless of where we might aspire to be, we are always in exactly the place we are supposed to be. Each choice we have made throughout our lives has brought us to this very moment. There is nothing more powerful and empowering than recognising this, while also honouring our true nature, standing in our truth and revealing our authentic self as it exists in this very moment.

I have a sense that the next great frontier awaiting exploration for humanity is not outer space, but inner space.

Creating Space

Those who know do not speak;
those who speak do not know.
– Lao Tzu

We have uncovered the myth that leadership is about communicating a vision. The problem with this myth is that
it focuses primarily on broadcasting a message (opinions) rather than on something much more important: listening.

Listening is the primary gateway to co-sensing and co-creating
the emerging future. The world is full of grandiose leadership visions
that were beautifully communicated – before they crashed and
burned. Think Enron, Lehman Brothers, AIG. The problem was not
a lack of vision. The problem was that the vision was completely out
of touch with reality. The problem was a lack of listening.

Otto Scharmer of the *Presencing Institute* describes four levels
of listening:

- Downloading – listening from habit. In this mode, you
  are on automatic pilot, just reconfirming what you

already know. You assume you already know what is being said, so you are in fact reinforcing old opinions and judgements.

- Factual – listening from outside. Now, you are opening your mind and discovering new information. By paying attention to what is novel, disquieting or different from what you already know, you are able to collect new data.

- Empathetic – listening from within. In this mode, you are opening your heart to see something through another person's eyes. Able to set aside your own agenda, you can focus on building an emotional connection. This in turn opens the listener and shifts attention from the listener to the speaker, enabling a deeper connection between the two people.

- Generative – listening from source. At this level, you are opening your will, meaning you listen in such a way that everything slows down and inner wisdom is accessed. In group dynamics, this can be referred to as synergy. In interpersonal communication, it can be described as oneness and flow.

I recently travelled to Istanbul for the first time. On arrival, I headed out to see the whirling dervishes at Hodjapasha. As the dervishes began to spin faster, I became mesmerised by the 700-year-old ritual. The dancers appeared to float between two worlds, falling into an intensely meditative state just by focusing on the 'now' of their whirling. I shared in their apparent joy in this experience of feeling themselves as the still point at the eye of the storm – as if they were the unmoving centre around which the whole world was spinning. They somehow looked so peaceful, despite their whirling.

The next day I took the ferry from Kabataş to the Princes' Islands. After a week of public speaking, I had practically lost my voice and I had forgotten to bring my headphones with me. With no distractions available, I was left to connect with the 'now'. And that was a challenge. The ferry was chaotic – it was as though the passengers wanted to play an hour-long game of musical chairs with some selfies thrown in. I felt unsettled, and yet amid the din sat a lady who appeared to be at complete peace in the chaos, rather like the dervishes in the centre of their own private storms. Impervious to the noise, she seemed to have reached a meditative state by knitting and occasionally looking up to notice the beauty of nature passing by. It got me thinking how rarely we connect to the silence within, which is what makes it possible to appreciate fully what is outside ourselves too.

Brain imaging studies show that technology stimulates brains just like cocaine does. It is addictive because it increases dopamine levels (the 'feel-good transmitter') as much as drugs or sex. Numerous researchers now use terms such as 'electronic cocaine', 'digital heroin' and 'digital pharmakeia' (drugs). It is the chemical need for the next hit that feeds the selfie culture, with photos having to perform best in an instant (#bestlife #bestdayever #nailinglife...). We have become used to having our senses stimulated all the time. I have seen people spend entire long-haul flights taking snaps in various poses, using the in-flight Wi-Fi to refresh likes, instead of using the time to disconnect and delve into the on-board entertainment, read a good book or catch up on some rest. Even Steve Jobs would not allow his children to have the very invention he created – the iPad. He knew!

In a joint study from the universities of Virginia and Harvard, scientists left individuals alone in a room for six to fifteen minutes without music, reading material, the chance to write or their smartphones. They were left solely to their own thoughts. The participants ranged from 18 to 77 years old and were drawn from a variety of social backgrounds, yet the results were the same regardless. Most felt discomfort and reported that it was very difficult for them to concentrate during the minutes they spent alone. The scientists then took the study one step further in order to see whether the participants would rather do something unpleasant, such as receive an electric shock, than continue the silence. Each participant had been subjected in advance to a similar electric shock so they would know exactly how painful that option was. And it was painful. Nevertheless, nearly half of the subjects eventually pushed on the button to administer an electric shock in order to reduce their silent time.

Over 20 years ago, a psychologist, Arthur Aron, ran an experiment where he had participants sitting and looking into each other's eyes without saying a word for up to four minutes. In one of the most widely read articles of the *New York Times* in 2015, the journalist Mandy Len Catron, who tried out Aron's theory and practice, wrote:

> *I've skied steep slopes and hung from a rock face by a short length of rope, but staring into someone's eyes for four silent minutes was one of the more thrilling and terrifying experiences of my life. I spent the first couple of minutes just trying to breathe properly. There was a lot of nervous smiling until, eventually, we settled in. I know the eyes are the windows to the soul or whatever, but the real crux of the moment was not just that I was really seeing someone, but that I was seeing someone really seeing me. Once I embraced the terror of this realisation and gave it time to subside, I arrived somewhere unexpected.*

Several studies have illustrated the value of spending time alone in solitude. Taking time for silence restores the nervous system, helps sustain energy, and conditions the mind to be more adaptive and responsive to the complex environments in which so many of us now live, work and lead. Duke Medical School's Imke Kirste recently found that silence is associated with the development of new cells in the hippocampus, the key brain region associated with learning and memory.

> While we are sitting in meditation, we
> are simply exploring humanity and all
> of creation in the form of ourselves.
> – PEMA CHODRON

For many, the 'great lockdown' taught the importance of taking a break, working less, and spending more time at home or in solitude so we can tune in to our inner selves. Social distancing and self-isolation allowed us to reset and reconnect. It is in that space of doing nothing at all that we discover the important things in life.

Is busyness bad for business?

A few years ago I worked with a client in Asia, and within a couple of days I sensed a pattern emerging. In response to 'Hello, how are you?' I would get the response 'Busy'…'Busy week ahead'…'Oh, you know, busy'…'Good, thanks – the weekend is in sight; just heading to my next meeting, which started two minutes ago.' Leaders in that system seemed to ascribe value to busyness. It was a proof of legitimacy, or at least it was a ticket to the game. I wonder: if we replaced the word 'busy' by 'ineffective', what might shift in that company?

Having led global teams in a matrix environment, I know what the demands on leaders' time can be like. When everything around me was moving so fast, I learnt to stop and ask, 'Is it the world that's busy, or is it my mind?' I realised that I was wearing busyness as a badge of honour, trying to justify my title and salary, and proving that I was doing my part.

Many of us are addicted to busyness, often as a numbing strategy. We do not see this as a problem because we call it being conscientious. If we are to realise our potential, then we have to embrace letting go of the need to control, to allow our mind to take a break and our ideas to flow. A busy mind has never been a fertile ground for innovation. Embracing an element of nothingness allows us to balance and produce more value.

Slow down – and see

While breaks are countercultural in most organisations and coun-terintuitive for many high achievers, their value is multifaceted. If business is about people and leadership about service, then it is important that we are grounded and able to hold space for others. Just as our body needs rest after a workout, our mind needs time to unwind, regenerate and recuperate. It is a skill to still the mind and think well. It is believed that managers influence 70% of team engagement, and they need time in their day to focus on that.

What has typically been viewed as useless daydreaming or mind-wandering is now being seen as an essential experience. Professor Jonathan Schooler, from UC Santa Barbara, says, 'Daydreaming and boredom seem to be a source for incubation and creative discovery in the brain.' When we are not focusing on anything in particular (passive rest), the brain's 'default mode network' (DMN) is lit up. The DMN usually involves thinking about others, thinking about oneself, remembering the past and envisioning the future. Indeed, many of our most original insights arise from the activity of this network. Istanbul reminded me that it is good to be bored sometimes. The hubbub of the world disappears when we still ourselves into inner silence.

What is needed from us all, now more than ever, is to be present and find the stillness to get into level-three and -four listening. It sounds easy, but in reality it can be the hardest thing we do. Otto Scharmer goes on to describe four sources of distraction that are pulling at us in every given moment.

The first one, we are all familiar with. It's called the past. When our attention, our thinking, is trapped by regretting what happened yesterday, by replaying conflicts, by wrapping our mind around what we could have said or should have said, we get stuck in that space. Ultimately, it draws us away from the sources of what is wanting to emerge.

The second one is called the future. When we worry about tomorrow, we lose our connection to the present moment. The only thing that is real is the present; the past has happened and slipped away, and the future is yet to unfold. The only point of access to reality we have, the only way we can shift how reality unfolds, is by connecting to our present moment, by connecting to what's emerging from the now.

There are two more distractions. The third is, 'It's all about them.' This is a mindset that we apply when engaging with other people and seeing them as the source of all our problems without seeing our own part in those problems. 'It's all about them' locates the source of issues outside us, typically leading us to lose our connection with ourselves. The fourth distraction is the opposite, which is of course, 'It's all about me', and is the flipside of the same process. In this space, we are overly consumed and absorbed by what may happen to us in this or that situation.

So those are the four sources of distraction. Since we need to deal with aspects of the past, the future, other people and ourselves, the question is: how do we engage with these things from a healthier, more insightful space? It will require the space and time to bring ourselves into full presence in the 'now', a space in which we are aware of our own thoughts and actions and other aspects of the bigger picture.

From there, we move into a connection with the past that we can describe as learning from those experiences while keeping sight of our own role in what happened. What if we were to apply the same mindset when leaning into the future, the space of possibility around us that is wanting to emerge or that could happen? If we use the same mindset to connect to others, we can collapse the boundary that separates us from them. It is a way of paying attention to ourselves by turning around the camera through which we usually view others and focusing it on ourselves, seeing ourselves from the larger sphere around us.

All great leadership starts with listening. That means listening with an open mind, heart and will. It means listening to what is being said as well as to what is not being said, and to the latent needs and aspirations of all people.

Our threshold for finding silence and balance can be lowered – getting inside what we are doing, allowing each moment to be big enough without searching for external stimuli. It is available even when we are surrounded by constant noise. We do not need a course in silence or relaxation to be able simply to pause. Silence can be anywhere, anytime. It is always there inside ourselves.

That is what changes us – creating a space inside for a new way of being to emerge, entering the realm of possibility and gaining insights into the pathways to the future that are calling us. It is there we find meaning and purpose.

Finding Meaning and Purpose

It always seems impossible until it's done.
— NELSON MANDELA

et's say you are living your life and the angel of death comes to you and says, 'It's time to go,' and you say, 'But no, you're supposed to give me a warning so I can decide what I want to do with my last week.' Do you know what death will say to you?

I've given you your whole life. How were you not aware that your time is limited and you're supposed to be using it for something meaningful? I gave you 52 weeks this past year alone, and look at all the other weeks I've given you. Why would you need one more? What did you do with all of those?

If asked that, what are you going to say? 'I wasn't paying attention'? 'I didn't think it mattered'? That is a pretty amazing thing to say about your life.

Most people wait until the second or third act of life to assess their legacy. What if we were to structure our decisions right now based on how we want to be remembered?

Every one of us is born with a purpose to fulfil in this lifetime – a special role in humanity. There is no one else on the planet who is here to be who you are and give what you have to give. Purpose is there all the time, and it is always calling you. Entelechy, from the Greek *entelecheia*, means 'that which turns potential into reality'.

Entelechy is inside you, like the butterfly is inside
the caterpillar...it is the entelechy of an acorn
to be an oak tree, of a baby to be a grown-up,
of a popcorn kernel to be a fully popped entity,
and of you and me to be God only knows what.
— TEILHARD DE CHARDIN

What is your reason for being?

In order to create more value for ourselves, for others, to advance humanity, we need to embrace our uniqueness. That is the fountain of creativity. Each of us has work to do in our contribution to the whole. One brick is not better than another because it is bigger or higher up in the building.

Purpose does not need to be grand. It is about understanding our unique talents and using them to bring happiness to others and ourselves. For inspiration, we might look to *Ikigai*, a Japanese word that translates simply as 'reason for being'. It is the sweet spot between that which you love, that which you are good at, that which the world needs and that which you can be paid for.

Bridging self with service brings an immeasurable amount of fulfilment to our jobs, relationships and the vision we have for our best life. In *The Power of Myth*, Joseph Campbell coined the phrase 'follow your bliss'. Campbell studied all human stories, mythologies and religions and this was his advice to us: pay attention to those moments when you are lit up, when time just flies by, and then use them to serve the world. So instead of, 'What can I get? How can I take? How can I manipulate?' the question is, 'What can I give?' When we freely share our gifts with others, we really give back to ourselves.

Ask yourself:

- What are the three most important challenges that your life presents?
- What are the three most important strengths or qualities that you bring to your work?
- What areas of interest or aspirations do you want to put more focus on in the future?

- What are your most vital sources of energy, what do you love, what gives you bliss?
- In your present self, what do you need to pay attention to in this moment?
- What would your future wise self want from you at this moment?
- How can you benefit others through your leadership?
- What do you want to be remembered for?

Living in wonder and making magic

Every life is filled with potential and meaning. But the system wants us to be blind to wonder.

Children look with wide-eyed wonder at practically everything. What happened to make us stop seeing our stories as wonderful? We trained our brains to ignore the familiar where any two days are more alike than different.

Open yourself to the possibility of perceiving and feeling your world differently. For example, two people can look at the same chair, but where one sees just a rickety old rocker with the arms coming unglued, the other is inspired to reflect on how the chair's life has led it to this point. The chair is the same, but the two people's perceptions have turned it into two very different experiences. By increasing our awareness we can start to notice things and gain experiences we did not have before.

To see how much potential is available in every second, just look at the room around you. Instead of seeing what you always see, consciously see three new things. It could be the angle of the sunlight, the expressions of people or the details in the carpet.

We are all wonderful (full of wonder). It is just that we have forgotten.

Share your vision; speak your truth

Being intentional about our purpose inspires action. What we speak comes to life, sparking collaborative potential and igniting possibility. The spoken word is a powerful tool, and by leveraging our voice we expand our dreams from internal thoughts to external possibilities. It is through our willingness to communicate and share ideas, perspectives and vision with others that we grow more comfortable being in and speaking our truth.

> Open to me, so that I may open. Provide me
> with your inspiration, so that I may see mine.
> – RUMI

When I was younger all I wanted to do was fly. Because my core value is freedom, being cooped up in a cockpit was unthinkable, so I opted for being cabin crew instead. As a kid, I would constantly be reciting public announcements on my voice recorder. I even created boarding passes for my family to get into the house, and would serve them 'minute meals' seated in pairs in front of the TV.

My parents wanted the best for me, and worried about me 'making it' in life. With a first-class degree and the opportunity to be a career diplomat, it seemed as though I was wasting my potential, especially since my contemporaries were entering flash corporate graduate programmes. But on my quest for a goalless life, I intuitively knew to follow the things that brought me the greatest joy, and my happiness would create ripples of good that emanated from within.

The ego mind will naturally want to know all the details ahead of time. Where exactly are we going? How long will it take? Will we succeed in achieving our desired outcome? We ourselves create the need for certainty and control, yet life is inherently uncertain and cannot be controlled. Relinquish your attachment to the result – I call this 'engaged indifference'.

I went sightseeing on this long journey to enlightenment, needing to go through every single experience to bring me to this point.

Like the line from the film *Slumdog Millionaire*: 'D: It is written.'

Life knows your purpose better than you do

The beauty of purpose is that it is dynamic and continues to be applied throughout our lives. Every day brings us a chance to start again. Although when you lose what you thought was a perfect relationship, when the job that defined you for 20 years is gone, when the people you counted on turn their backs on you, it can be hard to imagine that you may actually be taking a step forward on the path to your truest desires and ultimately to your destiny. Everything that happens to us is a means to help us evolve into who we are meant to become. Perceived failure is just life trying to move us in a different direction and bring us more of who we are. We move in the direction of the life for which we are intended.

By opening ourselves to uncertainty, even if just a little bit at a time, we gradually release self-imposed limitations and allow our life and journey to unfold in ways that are more wondrous and fulfilling than we could ever have imagined. No matter how far we stray away from ourselves, there is always a path back. We come to realise that there is nothing we can lose that will diminish our wholeness, and nothing we can gain that will add to who we are. You are already whole, as is the rest of humanity.

In a world that seems ever more complex, it is time for us to reconnect with our humanity. True purpose is not about acquiring anything – it is about evolving yourself. It is the possibility of change through shedding layers and becoming more conscious, more compassionate...more you.

Years ago, Oprah Winfrey interviewed a grieving mother whose adult son had died following a long illness. You could have heard a pin drop in the studio when the mother recounted the story of their final moment together. The mother had climbed into bed with her son. She could barely hear him, but her head was on his chest. As he took his last breath, he whispered, 'Oh Mom, it is all so simple. It's so simple, Mom.' He then closed his eyes and died.

Letting go of that which no longer serves

For centuries, the First Nation and Native American people of the Wabanaki Confederation literally had to carry their homes on their backs whenever they had to migrate. Known as 'portaging', this process involved their carrying a canoe or boat and all its contents across land from one body of water to another. Portaging, then, partly refers to the process of choosing what to take and what to leave behind as one makes the journey forward in life.

What a beautiful concept – to carry forward only that which serves your highest good.

My hope is that you drop anything that weighs you down – needless doubt, perfectionism, entangled relationships – whatever it may be. As you navigate the currents of these pages, what do you choose to leave behind? Your answer to that question is the next step on your path.

When you let go of the stories that no longer serve you, you create a new story with endless possibilities. And what a beautiful possibility you are.

Just imagine what lies around the bend. Can you see it? I can.

Time for Humanity

The awakening of consciousness is the
next evolutionary step for mankind.
– ECKHART TOLLE

When Michelangelo was asked how he created the finest sculpture on earth, it is said that he replied, 'I didn't create him. All I did was chip away at the marble that wasn't David.' In other words, David was always within the block of marble, he just needed to be revealed.

We start acquiring layers from an early age as we learn to conform. It starts during the imprint period as children, and carries through to our corporate careers. We are not even aware that we are conforming to invisible forces that are designed to control us and keep us asleep. To break free from these old chains around our being, we begin by going within and seeing what we need to edit out of our programming, taking inventory on the judgements and programmes which are running us and of which we are not even aware. We will inevitably see that we have been masking ourselves in order to survive in the system – essentially, dimming our humanity. It is time to stand up, be willing to unlearn in order to relearn and peel off our layers to reveal our humanity...to be our true selves.

The endless subcategorisation and labelling in which we have lately been encouraged to participate is creating a fragile illusion of rights, in which we are lured into separating out from one another. This process takes us ever further from our collective humanity. We have been unconsciously colluding in the 'divide and rule' agenda of a powerful elite, as we become distracted by all this fighting among ourselves. Definitions always leave things out. Though we do not look or act the same, at our core most of us want the exact same thing: to be treated with dignity and given the opportunity to express our unique self – each character trait – and to bring our genius to this world.

If you're not careful, the newspapers
will have you hating the people who are

> being oppressed, and loving the people
> who are doing the oppressing.
> – MALCOLM X

We are at a pivotal point in history. The question of whether we want to remain human needs to be placed against the transhumanist alternative – the desire to 'transcend the human' by merging with tech, at the expense of our human souls. Our choice is either to regain our humanity and grow it, make it great again, or to go down the AI-enhanced human route the system intends for us all. The choice we face comes down to the power of love, or the love of power.

It occurs to me that if you are part of a power structure that you have recognised as oppressive in any way, there is the real possibility of your cutting your shackles one day and speaking the truth. Power comes from the perception of power. The secret lies in people respecting and fearing it. Once they no longer believe in it, the power is gone.

The seeds for transformation lie in seeing our reality more clearly, without preconceptions and judgements. When we learn to see our essential part in humanity, we begin to develop a different relationship with our 'problems'. We are no longer victims. We become open to what might be possible, and we are inevitably led to the question: 'Who do we consciously choose to be and what do we want to create?'

The problem is us; therefore, the opportunity is us

When we look at the entire set of disconnects as a whole system, we see ourselves. The problem is us. It is we who burn resources beyond the capacity of our planet to regenerate them. It is we who participate in economic arrangements that replicate the income divide and the consumerism and burnout bubble that come with it.

The key feature of morality is the transition from 'I' to 'we'. The journey from 'ego-system' to 'ecosystem' means addressing the root causes of disruption to business, society and the environment. We are guilty of the silo mentality that addresses the problem at the symptom level but largely misses the interdependency across this and every other problem. We have the opportunity to recontextualise our relationship to the whole. After all, to own oneself completely is to own all of humanity.

We are leaving transactional, hierarchical, bottom-line-focused leadership behind. Our collective role in creating a more inclusive, equitable and regenerative economic system for all people and the planet has never been more important than it is now. The change has been emerging in an organic way from the edges. It is time to use the power of business to solve social and environmental problems, rewiring the way businesses are governed, managed and led, and changing how they define value and understand their role in society.

And if you will not step up, then who will? If not now, then when?

Sister Joan Chittister was 12 when she came home and her little parakeet was gone. She was an only child and the bird was her companion. She did not go home to playmates, she went home to Billy. And now Billy was missing:

My father moved every piece of furniture in that apartment. My mother looked under every chair. I got into bed and I sobbed. I knew I had to be quiet. I couldn't disturb anybody. But I was crying, my little body heaving. And the next thing I knew was I felt someone on the floor beside me, and then an arm on my back, and I realised it was my mother. And then I felt somebody on the floor on the other side, and I realised it was my father, and they had their arms around me saying, 'That's all right, darling. We understand. That's all right.' As I look back over the years, that's when I learnt that humanity is about identifying with somebody else's pain. Humanity is the ability to hurt for others. Because that's the only fuel that will stop the injustice.

While the path ahead is almost certainly connected to the deeper dimensions of our humanity – 'What is the purpose of life? What is the value of life? Why do we exist?' – we need to recognise the role we play in the system and adjust our approach accordingly, remembering that humanity is not singular; it is plural. This is the moment for humanity to reclaim its power and raise its vibration.

It's #time4humanity.

There is no such thing as an ending,
just a place where you leave the story.
And it's your story now...You have no
idea now what you will become.

Don't try and control it. Let go; that's when the
fun starts. Because as I once heard someone
say, there is no present like the time.
— THE SECOND BEST EXOTIC MARIGOLD HOTEL

Printed in Poland
by Amazon Fulfillment
Poland Sp. z o.o., Wrocław

60733500R00114